PRO TACTICS™ SERIES

PRO TACTICS™

ICE FISHING

Use the Secrets of the Pros to
Catch More and Bigger Fish

Jason Durham

THE LYONS PRESS
Guilford, Connecticut
An imprint of The Globe Pequot Press

To buy books in quantity for corporate use
or incentives, call **(800) 962–0973**
or e-mail **premiums@GlobePequot.com.**

Copyright © 2009 Morris Book Publishing, LLC

ALL RIGHTS RESERVED. No part of this book may be reproduced or transmitted in any form by any means, electronic or mechanical, including photocopying and recording, or by any information storage and retrieval system, except as may be expressly permitted in writing from the publisher. Requests for permission should be addressed to The Globe Pequot Press, Attn: Rights and Permissions Department, P.O. Box 480, Guilford, CT 06437.

The Lyons Press is an imprint of The Globe Pequot Press.
Pro Tactics is a trademark of Morris Book Publishing, LLC.

Thank you to the Minnesota Department of Natural Resources for their kind permission to reprint its safety recommendations for anyone who falls through the ice. See chapter four.

All interior photos by Jason Durham unless otherwise credited

Text design by Peter Holm (Sterling Hill Productions) and Libby Kingsbury

Library of Congress Cataloging in Publication Data is available on file.

ISBN 978-1-59921-367-5

Printed in China

10 9 8 7 6 5 4 3 2 1

The author and The Globe Pequot Press assume no liability for accidents happening to, or injuries sustained by, readers who engage in the activities described in this book.

To our ancestors who passed their ice fishing
information down to later generations,

and to the late Oligney,
who always had an extra seat in his Scout.

■ Lakes containing ample amounts of forage support larger numbers of walleye and provide the food needed for fish to mature and reach their maximum size. In-Fisherman Professional Walleye Trail director Chip Leer displays the pinnacle of winter walleye fishing. COURTESY CHIP LEER

CONTENTS

The Legacy of Ice Fishing

Ice fishing is not simply a pastime or professional endeavor, it is my heritage. Angling wasn't a late-life introduction or an alternative to risky adolescent activities. I started fishing, or at least accompanying my parents on excursions, from birth. It's simply what we did.

My earliest recollections of ice fishing date back to the age of about four, and I can still envision the greenish illumination

■ Winter's chill is temporarily forgotten while seated inside an ice house. It's difficult to tell if these structures are occupied at first glance, but the tip-up lying flat on the ice in the lower left-hand corner is evidence that someone is inside, waiting to catch a big fish. BILL LINDNER

from the oversize ice hole that over-whelmed most of the dark house (our name for a fish house) floor. Our family never spearfished through the ice, but instead angled through a spear hole, enabling the occupants to watch each fish approach from several feet away.

The fish house wasn't big, 4 by 6 feet, but because the hole was so large, floor space was limited. There was a 1-foot-wide strip of flooring on each side of the hole, and to me that was the best seat in the house. A wooden crate tipped on end served as my stool, and my feet dangled over the water. Ironically, I never felt the risk of fall-ing in, but if a car or snowmobile passed, causing the ice to boom and crack, I would streak out the door, hyperventilating at the thought of sinking to the bottom. Even so, I'd always venture back into the fish house and return to fish with my father day after day, week after week, year after year.

It was our tradition to put the fish house out the day after Christmas. My dad was never interested in pushing the limits of the ice to get it out early, and I would stand and watch as he chiseled the hole by hand. His tool dated back generations, a hand-made, wooden-handled chisel with an added "bump" of weight on the steel head that caused me to wonder of its prowess as a whale harpoon. I suppose that at the time of its origin, whale harpooning was common practice in ancient Finland, my great-great-grandfather's native coun-try where this particular chisel was cre-ated. Then again, this was the thinking of

a seven- or eight-year-old child standing in the cold for an hour as his father methodi-cally trenched an outline of the massive, rectangular hole. Once completed, we'd slide the dark house over the hole, peering inside after every minor adjustment until the hole was perfectly in line. I would go back to that moment in a heartbeat.

After a number of years, the wooden fish house succumbed to weathering and rot. The frame was no longer solid and the walls were caving in. It was time to let it go. When Christmas came around, the thought of no longer stoking the tiny woodstove with cedar scraps from the local birdhouse manufacturing plant or staring through the crystal-clear water to a fasci-nating world below saddened me. Now we would be fishing open ice.

My dad and I walked the hundred yards or so from our house down to the lake on a brisk winter afternoon, pulling a gear-filled toboggan behind as we prepared to angle in the open; no fish house for pro-tection. Actually, he pulled and I watched. Sometimes I even rode along with the gear. Nevertheless, today there wasn't any playfulness, and I was mad. I could see the smoke rising from a fish house seated right in our honey hole! Typically, our fish house was the only one in the entire bay. Now some random guy, I thought, has put his shanty right in our spot. Shoot, he's prob-ably keeping every fish he catches, and I just know they're biting.

As we drew near, I could make out the owner's name and address on the house in

3-inch black lettering. Why did he put it here, I wondered, when he lives 15 miles away and there are plenty of good lakes between those two points? In fact, there were nearly a hundred lakes within a 10-mile radius of our residence.

I told my dad that I was angry. He didn't say much to calm me down, but instead began hand-augering a couple of holes for us to use. After more fuming and little success to show for our effort, my dad hatched a plan. He thought we should go over to the fish house and ask the person what he was catching. Dad went over by himself; I wanted nothing to do with the trespasser.

He knocked once, twice, three times. The door never opened. My dad looked back at me and opened the door himself, peering in. "There's nobody in here," he exclaimed and motioned for me to come over. I hesitatingly approached, and he stepped inside. What is he doing? I wondered.

"C'mon, let's fish in here for a bit," he said and held the door open for me. It went against my better judgment, but when a father tells his son to do something, he does it.

So there we sat in some stranger's fish house. I was on edge, nervous, waiting for the owner to discover the two intruders, but at the same time, we were having a blast. There were fish of every species coming in to examine our baits, and we had several lying outside the door for dinner. After a while, my dad turned to me and said, "So what do you think?"

"About what?" I inquired.

"The fish house," he replied. "Do you like it?"

"Yeah, and he's got it in a really good spot," I said, coveting the owner's arrangement.

My dad caught another fish, then turned to me and asked, "Do you want to keep it?"

"Huh?" I was dumbfounded. Pretty naïve, too.

"This is our house," he said. My dad had bought the fish house and put it out on the lake unbeknownst to me, leaving the previous owner's name and address on the exterior as a diversion.

Year after year, my dad pulled that fish house onto the ice until I was big enough to lend a hand. When I was old enough to do it myself and opted to tow it halfway down the lake, he spent hours carefully chiseling out the house from 6 inches of frozen water, the flooding caused by an abundance of snow and a lack of responsibility on my behalf.

Today things have changed. Now my father and I spend most of our time on the open ice, cranking out dozens of holes with a gas auger and systematically probing each one with electronics, cameras, and baits that fish can't seem to resist. Retired after years of devotion to the United States Postal Service, my dad has enough time to explore new lakes and areas where we've never been, leaving our "honey hole" to other anglers interested in catching a meal.

Many anglers find similar beginnings on the ice. Although time and experience may change the angler's outlook and approach, in the end we all share a commonality—a vested interest in a unique pastime—ice fishing.

The basics of ice fishing are simple even for those who have never set foot on the arctic terrain of a frozen lake. Diversifying your technique, increasing mobility, and fully understanding what ice fishing entails is a process that takes time. But hopefully, after perusing the pages of this book, you'll gain insight to the sport, whether it's your first time or your daily venture onto the ice.

Many ice fishing aficionados who possess a high level of affection for angling amidst winter's fury have probably searched for an explanation for their obsession. Ice anglers share the experience of cold feet that make their legs feel like stumps instead of appendages, hands on the brink of solid ice, and core chills that inflict dizziness, but throughout it all, we stay out long past reason.

After the day concludes with a warm shower or welcome soak in the hot tub, the idea of returning to the frozen tundra of the northern lakes once again returns. Of course, we can all have a good laugh at some of the adversity, but what truly draws people out onto a frozen body of water and offers an experience that they become not only interested in, but also passionate about?

One reason might be that ice fishing isn't a feasible endeavor throughout all portions of the world. Chartered ice fishing trips simply aren't available on your January trip to Puerto Vallarta, Mexico. There's a camaraderie to participating in something that is so unique. Yet the majority of people who partake in the ice fishing season grew up in characteristically cooler northern climates. For these devotees, ice fishing isn't about doing something uniquely different, it's about sharing a pastime that most of their neighbors and acquaintances have experienced. Ice fishing is a communal passion that grows from the rooted infrastructure of family and friends, a social endeavor both on and off the water.

CHAPTER ONE

Getting Started

When you spend hours upon hours outside in freezing temperatures, literally *on* the ice, your first priority is staying warm and comfortable. Catching fish is the goal, so proper preparation in terms of clothing and considering the option of using a shelter will help you stay on the lake for longer periods of time—and therefore possibly catching more fish—despite the frigid conditions.

Clothing

Out of all the equipment available for ice fishing, proper clothing is the most important. You can carry along advanced electronics, a speedy auger, and irresistible baits, but if you get cold, the trip is over.

Dressing in multiple layers of clothing traps the most body heat, keeping you warmer longer. Removing extra clothing is simple; carrying additional attire along in a suitcase just in case you get cold is more difficult. The challenge is to stay just warm enough—breaking out in a sweat cools the body but leaves moisture on your clothing that will chill you afterward. Staying both warm and dry is the goal of any ice angler.

Thermal underwear is the first layer of defense against energy-sapping cold. Wool socks are great, but a number of synthetic materials rival wool's effectiveness. The key is to put your socks on *before* your thermal underwear to maintain a tight seal and to prevent them from sliding down your ankles and into your boots.

What you wear over your thermal underwear is all personal preference, but a few favorites stand out. For instance, lined wind pants fit comfortably over thermal underwear and provide both warmth and flexibility.

Hooded sweatshirts are another cold-weather favorite. They prevent wind from lashing at the angler's bare nape, and the hood doubles as an extra insulating layer, keeping your head warm over a stocking cap.

An ice angler's outer jacket and snow pants should be windproof and waterproof. Constant contact with snow, ice, and water demands a protective exterior barrier. Flying ice chips and water produced while augering a run of holes would soak a pair of jeans, ending the trip abruptly, or at least causing discomfort for the remainder of the day.

■ A baseball cap and sweatshirt may suffice on a warm winter day, but heavily insulated bibs, jacket, stocking cap, and gloves are required when the mercury plummets. Insulated outerwear that sheds water is ideal for ice fishing as damp clothing equals a cold angler. BRENT TOMMERDAHL

Gloves may serve the most important function, keeping your hands warm and dry. Ignoring cold feet is much easier than forgetting about frozen fingers. Mittens provide warmth on the journey to and from your fishing destination and while you drill holes, but once you take hold of the fishing rod, gloves are the only way to go.

Thick gloves provide warmth but get in the way of a spinning reel's bail and line guide. Thinner, form-fitting gloves pro-vide more flexibility, but you should care-fully examine their material content and construction before you buy. No matter how flexible they are, if the gloves aren't warm enough, the cold will leave you awk-wardly attempting to retie a broken line, or worse yet, fumbling with your zipper when it's time to go to the bathroom.

Jackets designed specifically for ice fishing have a windproof, waterproof exte-rior shell, plenty of insulation, and numer-ous pockets for storing miniature tackle boxes, matches, extra gloves, and hopefully, a little angling luck.

Waterproof bibs or overalls are mandatory for any ice angler, since contact with the snow and ice is constant and inevitable. Water sloshed from augering holes and the occasional wildly flopping fish would soak a pair of blue jeans, but ice fishing bibs keep the angler dry and warm. Some designs additionally have padded knees to alleviate the day-after pains from kneeling on the hard, frozen lake all afternoon.

Fish Houses

Fighting the elements is an ever-present aspect of ice fishing. Wind, snow, rain, sleet, and, of course, cold can restrict both mobility and enjoyment. Yet choosing the right fish house can be a feat in itself. Call them shanties, ice houses, dark houses, spearing houses, shacks, tents, or a multitude of regional references, but don't underestimate their ability to keep you warm!

Most important, an ice shelter breaks the chilling winter winds that can freeze your ice hole and cool your body. It also blocks rain, snow, and sleet, providing refuge from the elements. Some shelters have built-in seating, while others require a small chair or at least an overturned bucket, a primitive, yet functional solution.

When deciding upon a fish house, first determine how mobile you want to be when out on the ice. Certain portable fish house designs permit quick relocation, while others are more permanent, resulting in a greater amount of time to set up and move. Stationary houses don't allow for much movement at all.

Flip-ups

Flip-over-style houses are the easiest to haul, set up, and reposition. The base is essentially a deep sled that works well for hauling equipment and acts as a seat for the angler. Modern portable fish houses and flip-ups are constructed of canvas or other lightweight wind and waterproof materials attached to an aluminum frame. Some coverings incorporate insulated materials, along the same principles used to create cold-weather clothing.

When the wind blows or the temperature is simply too much to handle, the angler can flip a canopy over the seat base and fire up a propane heater to warm fingers and toes. The angler returns the top to the down position when ready to move to a new location, pulling the portable shelter along as a sled. Various models can accommodate more than one angler, but as the sleds get bigger and more canvas is required for the top, the weight increases and the shack becomes harder to move.

When using flip-over-style portables, pre-drill numerous holes in a large area before engaging in any angling. As the fish are located, drill additional holes in a smaller area where you have experienced the most success. Continually refining your area to target concentrated structural elements is an important strategy for catching more and bigger fish. By doing so, anglers can pinpoint attractive "spot-on-the-spot" locations that can quickly be saved on a handheld GPS and accessed on the next trip.

Suitcase Houses

Another shelter option is a portable fish house with a floor. Although these don't permit simple mobility, they do work well for getting out of the elements. Some portables have wood floors and fold in half like a traditional suitcase, although on a much larger scale. Others have molded bases created from heavy-duty plastic, formed to act as a built-in sled with runners that easily slide along the ice. Plastic frame houses are comparatively lighter than wood.

The advantage to having a wood floor is that the angler can create hole cutouts in any position, because the hole ports aren't pre-cut. The disadvantages include heavier overall weight and less mobility, and because the floors are wood, they can rot after several years of exposure to the weather. A common approach with suitcase-style portables is to first fish on the open ice to locate the most productive area. Once found, erect the fish house in the prime area. If the fish move, simply head back onto the open ice, periodically using the portable as a warming hut.

It is advisable to consider a set of fish house stakes for securing the structure in place if using a portable with a plastic floor. Once the occupants leave the shelter, rob-

bing the base of weight that enhances its stability, a swift winter wind can sweep the fish house across the ice faster than you can run without ice cleats. This is not a huge deal if you are fishing a 150-acre pond, but can present some problems when the ice spans miles.

Stationary Houses

Originally constructed for the purpose of spearing through a large hole, stationary houses today can be primitive structures or amenity-rich lodges. Also known as dark houses, these fish houses were originally designed without windows and often painted black inside to absorb the available light so the angler could more easily see into the water below. Today some stationary houses have windows so the occupants can see to tie knots or even play a game of cards, although the original dark houses are still used by those desiring a clear view of what's taking place in the water below. Venture out on any frozen lake throughout the Midwest, and you'll see houses made of heavy wood, hauled onto the lake using handmade sleds with old water skis as runners. Plumes of smoke billow into the frosty gray atmosphere as the wood-fueled stove heats up the interior. Stationary fish houses offer great protection from Mother Nature, but unfortunately, their mobility is somewhat limited. A sore back and a dose of pain relievers usually accompany moving the structure even a few feet!

Wheel Houses

Fish houses on wheels are innovative, well-planned, multipurpose trailers that contain propane heaters, ovens, cabinets, bunk beds, electricity, and even bathrooms. Many of these fish houses are on specialized frames that raise and lower with little effort, and additionally double as portable hunting shacks. Certain models can even haul your ATVs while traveling.

Drilling holes for such large fish houses can be problematic without prior advice. Pre-augering holes before lining up the fish house will only result in frustration. Yet running a gas auger inside the house can produce noxious fumes while the bit churns shaved ice onto the carpet. Forty years ago, ice anglers would have laughed at the predicament, but today keeping your fish house carpet in good shape is a concern!

To remedy the situation, drop the fish house frame so the structure is in its "fishing" position. Using an electric auger like Jiffy's Stealth Lectric eliminates the potentially harmful emissions of a gas auger, and the specially designed ice house handles permit the user to drill holes close to fish house walls.

To solve the problem of ice chips landing on the floor, stop at a feed store and pick up a plastic water container used for small farm animals. Large buckets used to pot trees at greenhouses also work well. Cut a hole in the bottom slightly larger than the diameter of your ice drill. Before you open your hole, place the newly crafted guard on top of the ice hole, lining it up with the opening you've cut in the bottom of the container. Now the majority of your ice shavings will land in the container, enabling careful disposal of the contents outside.

Renting vs. Buying

Purchasing a fish house on wheels involves a sizable financial undertaking. Since many anglers don't have the monetary resources or simply don't spend enough days on the water to justify purchasing a decked-out fish house, another option exists—renting.

Many resorts and private companies rent out fish houses on large bodies of water, even for large groups of people. Typically, someone opens the holes and turns on the heat for you, so the only work left is to catch fish. Rental sources move these houses periodically to follow the best fish activity, eliminating the need to research fish location before your arrival.

Heating Your House

Your choices for fuel to heat your fish house are generally propane and wood. Talk with your local dealer about choosing the appropriate heater. Before you choose wood, however, be aware that it has its limits. Some local agencies don't allow bonfires on the ice for protection of water quality. And some private landowners aren't keen about strangers building fires on their land. Along that line, don't count on finding wood at your spot—it's best to haul it along with

■ Certain fish house designs accommodate easy transport. The wheels on this once-stationary shelter allow the owner to easily haul the structure using a truck or ATV, a welcome option compared to back-breaking manual effort.

■ Ice travel is made possible using snowmobiles or ATVs to pull heavy-duty molded sleds and portable fish houses. A custom cover enclosing the sled protects the angler's gear from snow expelled from the track of this snowmobile and additionally prevents unexpected equipment loss while traveling at high speed or over rough terrain. CHIP LEER

your other equipment and to haul out the ashes. Overall, respect the property owners and the water quality and environment that offer you great fishing.

Sleds and Storage

Hauling gear on the ice while traveling by foot is most easily accomplished using a sled. Even if vehicle travel is safe, pulling a small sled along as you walk from hole to hole provides simplicity and organization. Traditionally, sleds that school-age kids used for shooting down snowy slopes needed the addition of sidewalls, but today hauling gear onto the ice is achievable with specifically manufactured sleds.

Flip-up-style shelters use molded sleds as their base, providing an easy method for carrying gear. Smaller sleds work nicely if the angler's means of travel is primarily by foot. Specialty hitches are available for anglers opting to haul their sled with an ATV or snowmobile. A spring-loaded coupler on the hitch absorbs the shock from rapid take-offs and quick stops.

Five-gallon buckets are a staple of the ice angler. These inexpensive organizers can easily carry rods, tackle, and even fish. Bakeries, painters, and sheetrock contractors commonly have an abundance of buckets that end up being recycled and are a fraction of the cost of those found in retail stores.

A five-gallon bucket can also double as a seat and can help you stay afloat in water, if the worst happens and you fall through the ice. Flipping the plastic bucket upside-down above water traps air inside, providing buoyancy for the unlucky angler. However, in extreme cold, hypothermia becomes the greatest danger for survival. (Chapter four looks more closely at ice fishing safety.)

As easy and inexpensive as the five-gallon bucket may be, padded rod and equipment cases protect your investments even better and prevent hooks from snagging other objects like clothing. It's frustrating to try to free your jacket sleeve from a hook when your goal is to catch fish, not yourself. Small tackle bags, handy backpacks, and full-length ice drill cases provide organization and protection for virtually any ice fishing item you own.

■ An organized ATV complete with custom carriers for augers, fish houses, and gear is advantageous for the mobile angler. A utility trailer is used for hauling the four-wheeler to the lake access, but the ATV serves as your pack mule on the ice.

The Open-Ice Advantage

When the ice is thick enough to support four-wheelers, snowmobiles, and vehicle travel, the amount of equipment feasibly brought along on a trip increases. It's easy to haul a 20-foot wheel-house out on the lake on a well-maintained, plowed path through the snow. Yet the primitive experience of standing on the open terrain of a lake can be advantageous despite the weather.

Mobility has become a buzzword in the ice fishing world. Traditional ice fishing entails attracting fish to your position. This means setting up a base above the school's current position or along travel routes used for hunting forage. If you drill a hole in the right spot, then catching fish is much easier, but an unproductive area results in nothing. Since schools of fish periodically move, a stationary fish house set in a certain location might prove productive one weekend and fishless the next. This is where open-ice mobility becomes a factor.

Instead of waiting for fish to approach, now the chase is on! An angler fishing the open ice can move quickly from hole to hole, spending only a few minutes in each spot until a school of fish is located. It's no longer a waiting game.

Some lakes aren't accessible by vehicle or ATV, and a long walk through the woods calls for a stripped-down gear list. Leaving portable fish houses at home is common during the early and late ice periods, since there is greater opportunity for mild weather. In fact, leaving behind a large percentage of the equipment brought along during midwinter expeditions simplifies mobility early and late in the ice fishing season.

An auger, scoop, flasher, rods, reels, and bait/tackle are your only requirements to fish, lightening the load while increasing your speed and mobility on the ice.

Finding Fish on the Ice

Set out on practically any body of water throughout the Midwest near dark, and it seems as though the carnival is coming to town. Trucks pull in and swiftly unpack mountains of gear, constructing temporary base camps that disappear a few hours later, when the bite slows following twilight.

Some anglers use concrete knowledge gained by electronic assistance, employing the use of underwater cameras, flashers, and GPS systems. These devices (covered in chapters two and three) can lead you to specific areas, indicate the presence of fish, and even identify the species. Just as important, these products can help you determine where fish are not, steering you to more promising areas.

Maps, state agencies, and word-of-mouth sources—both local and online—are other good information sources for where to find fish.

Maps

The most economical resources for examining potential fish-holding structure are lake maps. Many can even be accessed free

■ These anglers realize the advantage of mobility while fishing on the open ice, but when arctic weather hits, the warmth of a shelter tempts even hard-core enthusiasts.

of charge online. Minnesota, for instance, has topographical lake maps available for viewing on the Department of Natural Resources Web site (www.dnr.state.mn.us). You can locate Web sites for additional states with an active Department of Natural Resources office by replacing the "mn" with the intended state's abbreviation.

Listening to Experts

Bait shop personnel have always been a reliable source of information when it comes to locating fish of any species, especially on bodies of water that entertain large numbers of anglers. Since the retail doors are constantly revolving with anglers, they receive quite a bit of information on a daily basis. Be advised that the information received is broad in nature, and you'll still need to incorporate common sense with mobility.

Local fishing guides are another resource. Many are personable and enjoy chatting about fishing in general. They'll often point you in the right direction and lend some valuable insight about bait selection, general areas, and slight nuances that equate to a successful trip.

Pre-trip planning can also take place via the Internet. Online maps and aerial photos provide general information for locating lake access and examining potential hot spots. Online outdoor forums offer up-to-date information from tech-savvy anglers. Some great sites include www.fishingminnesota.com, www.thenextbite.com, and www.Nodakoutdoors.com. These community-based Web sites often have information, such as ice conditions and hot lakes, and include instructional articles and streaming how-to videos.

CHAPTER TWO

Ice Fishing Gear and Equipment

At one time ice fishing may have been considered hard work, cumbersome and labor intensive, but with the advent of highly specialized and properly adapted ice fishing equipment, it has turned into a favorite season for many anglers. Who would have thought a specific group of anglers would lie around on a warm sand beach in July, pining for summer to end? Ice anglers do, and they are not afraid to admit it.

A certain amount of gear is required for ice fishing. Some items are necessities, while others make an outing more comfortable, convenient, and productive. Comparing ice fishing to golf, you can get out on the links with a couple clubs and a ball, but additional equipment and practice will aid your score. With fishing, a few items will get you on the ice, but specialized equipment can make it easier and help you catch more fish.

An Arsenal of Tools

Warm-weather anglers often categorize themselves as species oriented, stating which fish is preferred as a target. A unilateral approach has become increasingly popular as tournament angling has prompted proficient anglers to become specifically bass, redfish, or walleye pros. A walleye angler's tackle box looks dramatically different compared to a bass angler's compendium of lures. Yet the vast majority of ice anglers are multifaceted, possessing the proper accoutrements to catch a variety of fish types.

We'll consider specific strategies and gear for various fisheries in chapters five through nine, and also later in this chapter under "Rods and Reels" and "Lures and Baits." But first, let's look at a handful of basic items needed to outfit your ice fishing expedition for virtually any species.

Ice Drills

First off, and no matter which species you pursue, cutting through the ice to reach water is imperative. There is no way you can ice fish without doing so. There are many methods to accomplish the task, but to minimize effort and maximize time efficiency, gas-powered augers, otherwise known as ice drills, are the way to go. Power augers expedite the chore of drill-

■ Cutting through the ice is integral to the sport of ice fishing. Although chisels and hand augers get the job done, a gas- or electric-powered drill decreases the amount of time and effort required to finally drop a line.

ing a hole, providing more time for the angler to fish. Since mobility is such an important asset while ice fishing, an auger should be one of your first ice equipment investments.

Two-stroke gas augers are quite easy to operate and maintain. Consisting of a power head (engine) and bit (the actual cutting mechanism), power augers are one of the greatest equipment assets for an ice angler.

If you have never used a gas auger before, it might first seem a little intimidating. However, this piece of equipment isn't like a chainsaw that can potentially "kick" and inflict harm, and it doesn't have blades like a lawnmower to throw objects in a rapid trajectory. An auger is very simple and safe to operate.

Jiffy ice drills are a reputable choice for several reasons. First and foremost, the drills are reliable and efficient. A compression-release mechanism makes it easy to pull the starter rope, even for an angler small in stature.

Another welcome feature available from Jiffy is D-Icer Armor, a special coating that helps to prevent ice buildup. Anyone who has ever battled with auger blades and bits jammed with ice recognizes the benefit of having some protection from freeze-up.

Jiffy's STX series blades make cutting holes a breeze. With five different cutting surfaces, the STX blades tear through the ice with utmost efficiency. There is no

need to apply downward force on the auger because once the blades bite into the ice, they pull the bit downward on their own.

Hauling the auger out onto the ice doesn't need to be a cumbersome chore. Place it in a sled to easily drag along, or position the bit on the balanced "sweet spot" of your shoulder with the power head behind you. Once balanced correctly, the auger sits comfortably secured by one hand with little noticeable fatigue.

Gas augers can rip through the ice quickly, but understand that the bit does not dually function as an ice chisel. Even though some bits have a sharp "point" on the bottom, pounding the blades on the ice may cause misalignment or even permanent damage.

It's best to include a small can of premixed gas in your equipment pile, since running out of fuel for the auger is an error without remedy while out on the lake. A gallon gas can doesn't take up much room in a sled and, if you are able to drive out onto the ice, won't even be noticeable in the bed of a truck.

Speaking of vehicles, protecting your auger during travel to and from the lake is just as important as protecting it on the ice. Since your ice drill is powered by gasoline, be sure the gas cap and vent are closed tightly before placing both your auger and additional gas can inside the vehicle. Otherwise, you may discover an empty tank on your next trip, not to mention a puddle of gas in your truck bed, SUV carpet, or car trunk. Special cases are available that fit over the power head or the entire auger. These come in handy when traveling and when the auger is stored for the season.

Chisels

The most basic of ice fishing tools, a good chisel can pound out a hole and saves the trip when you pull out the auger to discover an empty gas tank, fouled spark plug, torn fuel line, or a combination of the three (some of the access roads can really throw the gear around in the back of the vehicle)—or, worse yet, that the auger's missing!

Actually, chisels are more popular for opening previously drilled auger holes. They are also a staple for anyone maintaining a fish-house spear hole used for angling.

A sharp chisel is comparable to a sharp knife. Both perform much better than a dull product. Years ago, chisels were created by forging the tip and attaching it to a wooden handle. Soon all-metal chisels were the norm. Today that same design remains popular, but multi-tiered, serrated tips rip through the ice with less effort.

Following the theme of portability, Feldmann Engineering, manufacturers of Jiffy Ice Drills, created a short, yet heavy-duty chisel called the Mille Lacs chisel. Named after the popular central Minnesota fishing destination (meaning "a thousand lakes"), the Mille Lacs chisel is pint-sized compared to standard models,

which makes it perfect for carrying in a five-gallon bucket.

Any smart angler realizes the potential for losing a chisel through the ice when putting strenuous effort into chopping a hole. Many models come with a ring welded to the top of the handle for affixing a short tether to wrap around the user's wrist. If not available, an electric drill can easily bore a hole through a solid metal handle for threading a rope through.

Dippers

Another oft-overlooked ice fishing accessory is a scoop, otherwise known as a dipper. Without a scoop, you'll succumb to rummaging through your equipment to create a makeshift dipper, or end up sifting the ice out with your bare hands. Jiffy's Chipper Dipper, coated with D-Icer Armor, prevents the buildup of ice as you clean out your holes. The unique tool doubles as a small chisel that can open recently frozen holes and has a measuring stick etched throughout the length of the metal handle, providing a simple way to check the ice thickness or measure a fish before release.

Fish-Finding Gear

In years past, it was common for anglers to hand-drill a couple of holes, set lines, and wait for the fish to arrive. Prospective fishing areas were simply the ones handed down from generation to generation, triangulated and often misjudged by landmarks. New anglers had to follow the snow-packed footprints from previous excursions, hoping they landed on worthwhile structure and a waiting school of fish.

Today things are much different. Ice anglers use flasher sonar to sound on precise locations of structure and fish. And landmarks mean little compared to the images and icons generated by a GPS (Global Positioning System) unit, yet another technical tool for aiding anglers in the search for fish. (We'll take a closer look at underwater cameras and the finer points of flasher sonar in chapter three.)

Flashers

Even today, some anglers view flasher sonar technology to be antiquated. It's true that flashers have a long history, but they are still the best option for finding depth, structure, and fish, and provide a real-time readout of your bait and what's additionally present below. Today's flashers have advanced in the areas of sensitivity, options such as interference rejection and zoom modes, and bright visual displays. These high-tech modifications (discussed in more detail in chapter three) make flashers one of the greatest assets an ice angler can own.

One of the most influential components of a flasher is the transducer. It can essentially make or break your success. The interior of the transducer contains a high-quality barium titenate crystal, and

the transducer's duties are two-fold. First, the transducer acts as a speaker and transmits an audible "click" repeatedly into the water. If you hold the transducer up to your ear with the unit turned on, you can actually hear the sound. The transducer's sound travels quickly while submerged in the water, much faster than through the air. This sound subsequently bounces off the bottom and returns to the transducer hanging through the ice hole. The transducer, which now acts as a receiver, intercepts the return "ping," transmitting the signal to the flasher unit where it transforms into a visual image. If the sound signal happens to encounter another obstacle before it gets to the bottom, such as a fish, weeds, a school of baitfish, or any type of protruding structure, the flasher's screen displays the image.

A flasher is your eyes beneath the water. All of Vexilar's FL-Series sonar flashers not only relay instantaneous information regarding fish activity beneath your ice hole, they also tell you what is *not* going on in the water. Confused? Years ago, anglers would hand-auger or chisel a hole and stare at the water, wondering what, if anything, was beneath them. Today mobility is much greater. With the advent of gas-powered augers, anglers can grind out a Swiss-cheese pattern of holes in a matter of minutes. Now people must decide whether they want to remain fishing in one hole when there are fifty others with similar potential. So many holes, so little

■ Flasher-style sonar units provide a real-time account of your current depth, bottom structures, and approaching fish. They are also super-sensitive and display even the smallest of baits.

time! Using a Vexilar FL-Series flasher, anglers can determine the presence of fish the very instant the Ice-Ducer is set into the frigid water. Yet the flasher is equally able to display nothing when there's *nothing* around. The absence of fish indicates a need for the angler to relocate. In other words, Vexilar FL-Series flashers optimize your time on the water—and minimize the guesswork!

This is not to say that sight-fishing isn't a worthwhile endeavor. The 8- and 10-inch holes that an auger bores are fine when using electronics. Yet sight-fishing inside a dark house with a larger hole can be both enjoyable and educational. Peering down a 3-foot by 2-foot opening through the ice opens up a whole new world of discovery and observation. Studying the mannerisms of fish and how they react to various baits and techniques is invaluable information that can help you land more fish even when you're not watching your opponent.

GPS

Although paper maps are an inexpensive general source of information on lake depths and landscape features, they become nearly obsolete in comparison to the advanced technology of a GPS.

Some handheld GPS units have mapping capabilities available on a data chip that displays depth contours and your immediate location in relation to those features. The chip provides a topographic map background on your GPS display, simultaneously charting your position in relation to the detailed depth contours. This technology eliminates the guesswork involved in locating structure. Think of all the times you've drilled countless holes while attempting to locate a sunken island, reef, or similar isolated offshore structure. A handheld GPS with a mapping chip directs you to the spot right away, providing more time to enjoy your hard-water voyage.

The GPS won't show everything, however, such as real-world obstacles that you often encounter on the ice—fish houses, ice heaves and pressure ridges, and other anglers. The GPS directs you to the general vicinity, but finding the specific spot, the "spot-on-a-spot," requires the assistance of your flasher.

Rods and Reels

Gone are the days of wooden "jiggle-sticks" and spike-tipped broomsticks. Manufacturers design ice fishing rods and reels specifically for cold-weather application. Yet a favorite reel used during the summer is equally applicable for winter use so long as the reel does not greatly outsize the rod. Rods, on the other hand, do not pull multi-season duty. Could you use a 6- or 7-foot fishing rod for ice fishing? Sure, but it's not a great choice. Short ice fishing rods put the angler in an ideal position for providing life to the lure and battling a fish. A long

4393284

■ The various designs of ice fishing rods serve specific purposes for certain applications. Pairing the proper reel to the shorter rods required for ice fishing offers peak performance, while a mismatched outfit functions sub-par, resulting in frustration. BILL LINDNER

rod would work just fine until you brought a hooked fish to the top of the ice hole, at which point you'd have to attempt to reach for the fish at a span of 6 or 7 feet!

Today's ice anglers don't bring a single rod and reel combo onto the ice, they bring several. After using and approving a well-suited outfit, many anglers purchase several similar combos. Since ice fishing rods and reels are smaller than open-water outfits, their price is substantially lower, making ownership of multiple rod and

reel combinations achievable even with budgetary constraints.

Premium ice fishing rods use identical materials for construction as their open-water counterparts. High-modulus graphite and flexible fiberglass cross over into hard-water application, as do superior components such as line guides, handles, reel seats, and hook keepers, but in smaller proportions. Most ice fishing rods are 18 to 30 inches, with some specialty rods available in shorter or longer lengths. As a rule, use longer ice rods for larger gamefish, since the length provides additional leverage and can absorb the shock from rambunctious predators. Some super-light longer panfish rods are popular with finesse anglers, since they can easily observe a bite while the soft tip gives little indication to the fish that an angler is looming above them.

Before purchasing an ice fishing rod, consider the environment of its use. The close quarters of a small, portable fish house require a short rod, since longer models would continually come into contact with the canvas walls, or worse yet, your propane heater.

Some manufacturers have developed super-sensitive bite indicators integrated into the tip design of the fishing rod. Primarily used for panfish, the spring bobber mechanisms eliminate the need for a float. However, in many cases, the bite indicator is only replaceable by purchasing a new rod or an aftermarket spring bobber specifically produced for adding to a fishing rod.

Pairing a like-size reel to balance the smaller, shorter rods used for ice fishing means many of your summer fishing reels will not work very well. Ultralight spinning reels can easily fit on an ice fishing rod, and baitcasting reels work on rods designed for larger gamefish, but the goal is to achieve the highest level of sensitivity and performance, the primary objective of a well-balanced rod and reel combination.

Baitcasting reels do not work as well as spinning reels in extremely cold temperatures. Water that clings to the fishing line is constantly retrieved into the reel, and on a baitcasting reel this means ice buildup in the oscillating line guide. Don't discount baitcasting reels altogether, because they do just fine in a heated fish house and when the ambient temperature is mild, but when the mercury plummets a spinning reel will perform much better than a baitcaster.

The spool of an ice fishing reel does not need to be very large since there will not be any long-distance casting toward structure. In many cases, almost exclusively with the exception of trout, a vertical drop of 40 or 50 feet is the maximum depth you will be fishing. You may not even go deeper than 20 feet in many instances. Nevertheless, don't be overly conservative when spooling up, no matter which species you are chasing. Lightning-fast runs generated by incidental encounters with pike, muskie, walleye, or bass require some extra line, so even if shallow-water perch or sunfish are your target, be prepared to tangle with a larger predator.

It wasn't so many years ago that the majority of ice anglers used a couple wooden pegs for winding and unwinding line instead of a reel. Fighting a fish with the line in your hands was common protocol. Anglers caught fish, but it wasn't long until they figured out a better system.

Today, ice fishing reels are manufactured for the modern ice angler. Cold weather pushes equipment to the limit. Moving parts struggle and stick due to winter's rage, but reel designs have progressed to provide easy operation in the

■ Large fish require heavier line, longer rods, and beefed-up reels. The baitcasting outfit shown is just right for a tepid afternoon, but extremely cold temperatures can cause some of the reel components to freeze up, in which case switching to a spinning reel better suits the environment. RON ANLAUF

elements. Yet even the highest-quality fishing reel will leave you disappointed without a properly adjusted drag. On the other hand, an accurately adjusted drag that's inferior lands you in the same situation. Losing a fish because of a maladjusted drag is simply angler error, but a malfunctioning drag results in defeat caused by equipment failure.

Selecting a reel with a good drag is not guaranteed even if you spend a little extra money. Stick with reputable brands, and consider bringing a short length of line along—6 feet is plenty—to test the drag before a purchase.

Once you have tied the test line to the spool and wound a few cranks of length, adjust the drag and slowly pull out the line. The drag should be smooth, and you should not be able to detect any increase or decrease in tension. The spool should turn easily with steadily increasing pressure on the line without requiring a sharp yank to get the rotation started.

Line

Monofilament line is the most widely used option for ice fishing. Berkley created two formulas, Cold Weather and Micro Ice, to accommodate the rigors of winter. Berkley Micro Ice line has a small diameter and less stretch than conventional monofilament, which in turn provides greater overall sensitivity. Berkley Cold Weather line remains flexible when exposed to the elements and resists freezing for longer periods. It comes in an electric blue hue

to provide easy visibility against a background of snow and ice.

Fluorocarbon lines have gained popularity by ice anglers, especially those fishing super-clear bodies of water. Berkley's Transition fluorocarbon is available in snow-contrasting shades of gold and crimson red, which change to a crystal-clear appearance once the line enters the water.

There is a decrease in ice buildup on both rods and reels while using fluorocarbon, since it does not absorb water. However, because of that same property, cinching a knot against the eye of a hook without lubrication can create enough friction to weaken the connection. Wetting the line in the water or with your tongue remedies the issue. Just beware of the hook when dampening the line with your mouth—ouch!

Fluorocarbon is an excellent choice while fishing lakes with superior water clarity or if targeting highly discriminatory fish. Originally fashioned for saltwater application, fluorocarbon has nearly the same light refractive properties as water, making it virtually undetectable by fish.

Superlines—tightly braided strands of material also labeled as "braid"—have gained popularity in the ice fishing world, particularly with the development of Fireline Crystal Micro Ice. Previously, anglers chose superlines for their minimal diameter and high tensile strength, but the product was opaque. Fireline Crystal is a transparent superline. Fireline Crystal Micro Ice is a good option for ice fishing

■ Conventional braided line and new-age superlines prove effective on the spool of a tip-up, holding up to the sharp teeth and powerful sprints characteristic of northern pike and other large fish. BILL LINDNER

and a definite step up from first-generation braided lines. Although it's not as clear as monofilament or fluorocarbon, Fireline Crystal unites the traits of monofilament and braid.

Some of the smallest braided superline strengths perform well on spinning gear for panfish. Because braided lines do not stretch, it is much easier to feel a fish delicately brush its lips against your bait. Larger sizes are applicable for larger gamefish, especially the toothy variety like northern pike. Spinning and baitcasting reels accept braided lines, as do tip-ups.

Nevertheless, no matter which size of braided line you select, a small amount of "backing" is required on the spool. Fourteen-to 20-pound test monofilament is ideal. Deciding to forgo the monofilament backing will cause some major problems while you fish. A tight knot won't even keep the line fixed in place, and most fish will cause the entire mass of wound line to slide around the spool while you reel.

Heavier superlines, 20- to 80-pound test, work well on tip-up spools, but you may want to consider a steel leader. Toothy pike and muskies combine raw, brute force with row after row of razor-sharp teeth. Even 80-pound-test braided line succumbs to stress when up against freshwater's wolves.

However, it doesn't make sense to attach leaders for "just-in-case" encounters

RE-SPOOLING BRAIDED LINE

The following steps will aid in the process of re-spooling with braided line.

1. Tie monofilament to the bare spool of the reel; 14- to 20-pound test is best. The more backing material used, the less superline required to fill the spool. Since superlines are substantially higher in price, conservation equates to savings. Yet you need to consider stripping a few feet of the superline periodically to ensure its integrity. Superlines don't develop memory or break down like monofilament, so a properly spooled reel won't need changing as often.

2. Connect your braided line to the backing material using a double uni-knot.

3. Fill the remainder of your spool with the braided line.

4. After extended use, strip a few yards of the braided line from the spool, cut, and dispose. This is necessary when the superline begins to look "fuzzy."

5. If connecting a monofilament or fluorocarbon light line leader to the business end, several knots hold fast, but in many cases a small swivel unifying the junction works better. Twisted superbraid is a nightmare, and a tiny swivel saves you from added frustration.

with a large fish while angling for bluegill, crappie, and perch. Thinking the leader will protect you from losing your tiny jig only results in fewer bites from panfish. Losing your jig won't matter if you are not getting any bites!

Lures and Baits

There is no way a person could generate a comprehensive list of hooks and lures for various fish types without some overlap. Bluegill like small jigs tipped with a maggot. So do crappie. And let's not forget

perch. See what I mean? Some baits cross over to other species, but the techniques differ slightly. Each subsequent chapter on the fish species most commonly adored by ice anglers offers suggestions for baits and worthwhile presentations.

Understand that the bait you decide to tie on will only work if there are fish present. This holds true no matter what species you're chasing and is one of the few finitely defined fishing facts. You cannot catch a fish in the bathtub, even while using the world's best, money-back-guaranteed, super-attractive fishing lure.

■ Many hooks, jigs, and lures are applicable for catching multiple fish species. These jigs could potentially land walleye, perch, or crappie, but a slightly smaller hook is required for the tiny mouth of a bluegill.

There is no magic bait that catches fish all of the time!

However, a general understanding of lures and presentation in conjunction with knowledge of seasonal fish movement and location completes a well-rounded package leading to more success.

Lure Color

Color, shape, and size are all important factors to consider when selecting a hook for any species. Since fish have color receptors in their eyes, presenting a color desired by the fish gains appeal. Human and fish visual perception is different in several ways, and fish probably do not see colors with the same saturation below water as we do on land. Ambient light decreases as depth increases, and a bait that appears as one particular color in your hand may look entirely different to a fish.

A well-known approach to selecting color suggests bright colors on bright days and dark colors on dark days. If bait selection were that simple, we would all have more photos on the wall of incred-

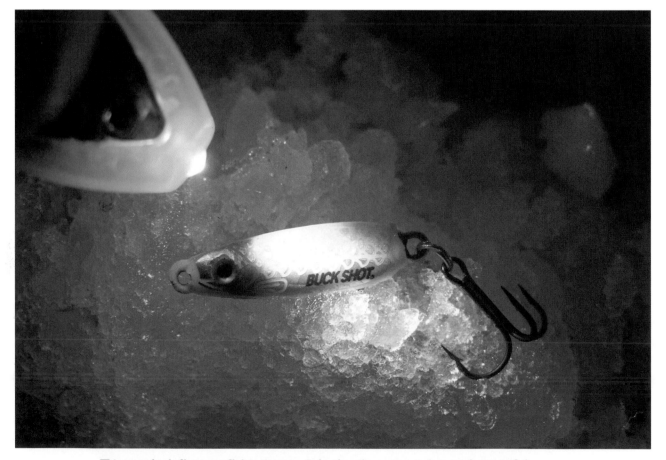

■ Lure color influences fish response. Selecting the proper color requires careful thought and unending experimentation. Some anglers prefer glow-in-the-dark baits charged with a Northland Glo-buster Lurelight for a unique underwater experience.

ible catches! Fish are frustratingly discerning one day and indiscriminate the next. Numerous factors influence a fish's response to color, including water clarity and natural forage types.

Both acutely natural and brazenly bold presentations can potentially prompt fish to bite. The first philosophy entails selecting lures based upon hues relevant to native forage. Colors like silver, copper, gold, black, white, and iridescent green appear most frequently on the backs, bellies, and sides of small minnows. Ice fishing jigs and lures that are painted realistically work particularly well in lakes containing clear water. This does not necessarily mean a naturally colored jig or lure will always work best in clear water, but it's definitely a good start. Natural colors also catch fish in dirty or stained water.

The second approach to color selection involves grabbing the fish's attention by offering bright-colored baits. Chartreuse, orange, hot pink, red, and fluorescent green contrast with the brown and olive drab backgrounds most commonly

■ Brightly colored baits stand out against the darkness below winter's ice cap. Light-blocking snow and ice dim the underwater environment, but fish still easily locate boldly colored jigs and lures both day and night.

found in lakes. Fish easily pinpoint the location of such baits and bite out of curiosity, reaction to movement, and hunger when they're active. Anglers often use bold colors when fishing lakes with low water clarity, since fish visually recognize the presentation from a greater distance, but sometimes a drastic color scheme is the answer in clear water. In other words, no concrete formula produces in every situation, so experiment.

As stated previously, water clarity has in immense effect on success. A fish must first locate your bait to eat it. Many anglers think of water clarity as water color, but clarity changes under the ice due to snow cover and the presence of sun and clouds. A secchi disc is the device typically used to measure water clarity throughout the summer months. The observer lowers this white "plate" into the water in 1-foot increments, continually focusing on the disc until it finally disappears, calculating depth upon retrieval.

Rays of light generated by the sun are absorbed in the blanket of ice and snow, decreasing visibility in even the most pristine lakes throughout the winter.

■ Eye placement dictates the resting position of these two baits. The Frostee (left) remains in an upright, vertical stance at rest, while the original Flyer hangs horizontally, an important consideration when deciding how to hook live bait for a natural appearance.

Horizontal vs. Vertical Baits

Anglers essentially present every ice fishing bait from a vertical point of origin. The resting position is horizontal if the body of the lure remains parallel to the bottom. Conversely, vertical baits sit with the body aimed straight up and down. The hook's eye position generally determines whether the bait will sit horizontally or vertically. I'm not talking about the eyes painted on the body, as they have no bearing on the balance of a bait, but instead refer to the eye of the *hook*.

A 90-degree bend in the structure of the hook will cause it to sit horizontally if the eye protrudes from the center of the jig body. The same hook design creates the skeleton of a vertical bait when its position extends from the front of the jig if the knot position from the angler's line so allows. Otherwise it ends up being somewhere between horizontal and vertical.

The bait's position becomes important when considering profile, shadow, and trailer action. The profile of a bait is the shape and outline from a side perspective. Some baits, like Lindy's Fat Boy, have a wide profile that gives the impression of larger forage even though the product is actually quite thin. From below, the Fat Boy may appear slender, but from the side it looks, well, fat. In brief, wide-profile baits emulate larger-size forage.

The bait's shadow seen from below encompasses the same philosophies as profile, but from another angle. Since fish often see objects from a bottom-up perspective and have visual fields that cater to that view, shadow and profile become equally important. Imagine an airplane as it prepares to streak down the runway. An onlooker can see the windows, round wheels, and the tail fin sticking up from the back. Now think about the same plane flying overhead as you look up from the ground. The prominent characteristics now include the wings, while hiding some of the earlier-noted features. Fish may not have the same visual abilities as humans, but perspective plays an important role in attracting fish to bite.

Horizontal and Vertical Trailers

The position of your hook, either vertical or horizontal, influences the action of your live bait or artificial trailer. Unfortunately, the influence isn't always positive. For instance, a delicately hooked minnow really drives big crappie wild, but where you place the hook will determine the minnow's position. If you are using a vertically situated hook, pierce the minnow through the back so it can swim naturally, positioned parallel to the bottom. Hooking the minnow through the lips will only cause it to hang vertically and limit its mobility. Yet if you're using a horizontally seated hook, like a Lindy Flyer or Genz Worm, the minnow could be effectively hooked through the lips and still maintain a parallel position in relation to the bottom.

Allowing a minnow to wriggle naturally puts a lot of fish on the ice. Yet certain baits, like jigging spoons, provide the action, so lively minnows are not necessary. Jigging spoons are an exception when it comes to hooking minnows. Even though the spoon itself sits vertically, you do not want to hook the minnow in the back. Doing so will only keep you reaching into the minnow bucket for more bait, even though a fish has yet to bite. Jigging the spoon with a back-hooked minnow causes too much resistance, and the hook will quickly tear free. Additionally, the minnow will limit the spoon's action. A lip-hooked minnow that aerodynamically trails the jigging spoon is a better choice.

Any worm variety is simple to hook. Either go just beneath the head, or thread it onto the hook. Plastic trailers such as Lindy's Munchies Tiny Tails have the same two options, but if you choose to thread a plastic-tail onto your hook, make sure it sits straight—either up and down on a vertical bait or parallel to the bottom when using a horizontal bait. If the plastic-tail isn't straight on the hook, your bait will gradually rotate as you jig. As it continually turns, any pause in your jigging results in the jig unwinding. Fish of any species don't tend to become aggressive toward

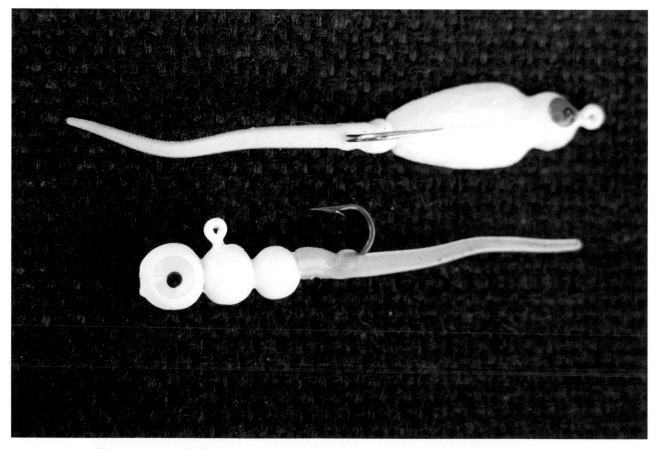

■ Both vertical (top) and horizontal (bottom) jigs benefit from the addition of a soft plastic-tail, although it's easier to make the tails dance while using a horizontally situated jig.

this action, and the outcome is a spool full of twisted fishing line.

Munchies Tiny Tails enhance the attractiveness of both horizontal and vertical baits, but horizontal baits allow easier production of action. When jiggled in conjunction with a horizontal bait, the plastic-tail whips like a flagellum, a naturally occurring forage action in an underwater environment.

Artificial Vegetation

Not long ago, some intuitive anglers at LaDredge Outdoors concocted an idea that at first seemed outlandish to others, but has now evolved into wisdom. In many states, sinking structure into a lake and leaving it there is illegal. Yet rumors would surface of anglers drowning brush piles or heaps of rocks under the blanket of night.

Now there is a legal, simple method to attract fish to an area. Reel Weeds, produced by LaDredge Outdoors, are synthetic weeds attached to a string and weight. This makes it possible to "plant" your own vegetation, even in areas where no weeds previously existed. Suitably named "structure on a string," the weeds are easily wound back onto a bracket at the end of the fishing trip.

A Few Accessories

Other than the basic items required to actually fish, a number of additional products simplify your experience. Some type of hook remover, for instance, comes in handy no matter which species you're after. Small forceps are great for reaching into the small opening of a bluegill's mouth, but the short-handled version makes hook removal from the incidental northern pike a headache. In most ice fishing areas, you have to plan for the species you want to catch and additionally plan to encounter northern pike.

A long-handled Baker hook-out is heavy-duty and can get your hook back from a toothy pike without risking a finger. Another good choice is the Gerber Fisherman multi-tool. The fast-tapered, needlenose pliers provide easy access to hooks inside any fish's mouth, while the accompanying tools—knives, screwdrivers, etc.—eliminate the need for an accessory toolbox. Cutting braided line, tightening a screw on a reel, opening the vent on an overtly fussy auger gas cap, stripping and splicing corroded wire, and numerous additional applications are all within the abilities of one tool that can fit in your pocket.

Walking on ice, especially an early- or late-season glaze absent of snow, requires ice cleats for both stability and safety. Several styles are available at both sporting goods outlets and footwear providers, but remember that you're fitting these over a pair of boots. Sliding them over your walking shoes in the store will only lead to a return. Extra-wide boots, like LaCrosse Ice Kings or military-issue bunny boots, might require extra-wide designs.

PRESEASON CHECKLIST

The following comprehensive checklist will help you have a successful, or at least incident-free, initial trip for the season.

Auger

- Check spark plug.

- Inspect fuel line.

- Refill gas tank.

- Examine blades for wear and integrity.

- Tighten bolt between engine and auger bit.

- Start the auger to ensure proper function *before* you get to the lake!

Rods and Reels

- Look over the rod and reel for signs of stress and wear.

- Check the reel seat for cracks.

- Rub the inside of your line guides with a cotton swab, specifically watching for spots that pull the cotton, indicating a rough burr.

- Remedy the defect by using a super-fine abrasive paper. If the issues are not self-repairable, replace with a new rod. When it comes to ice fishing rods, the difference in cost between professional repair and total replacement is typically even.

- Apply cold-weather lubricant to reels.

- Re-spool with fresh line.

Tip-ups

- Remove spindle and place a few drops of cold-weather lubricant in shaft.

- Check line for nicks and wear. Replace if necessary.

- Organize! Develop a system to prevent tip-ups from becoming a tangled mess.

Portable Fish House

- With the portable in a dark environment, place a light inside and walk around the exterior of the shelter. Light will show through holes and tears that may need repair.

- Make sure you have a current license for your fish house if required by state regulation.

Flasher

- Carefully examine transducer cable for nicks or cuts. If there's a slight nick on the outer cable covering, repair with tape or sealant. Shipping the transducer to the manufacturer's service department is required if a wire is cut.

■ **Carefully checking equipment long before the ice fishing season arrives leaves ample time to remedy defective gear. The cut in this transducer cable needs attention; procrastinating will lead to loss of fishing time.**

- Gently wipe the face of the transducer with a soft, damp cloth to remove any dust and dirt.

- Check the wires leading to the power supply. The connection between the wire and terminal connector is the area of highest susceptibility.

- Charge battery to full capacity.

Propane Heater

- Carefully examine propane cylinder for oxidation. Replace if necessary. *Never* use a sander or grinder on the tank, even if you think it is empty.

- Check hoses and valves for leakage.

- Fill propane tank.

Preseason Gear Preparation

Long before ice encompasses a body of water, good ice anglers start preparing for upcoming fishing trips. Procrastinating until you're already on the ice often results in sub-standard performance, yet a few preseason observations ensure that your equipment will operate properly once cold weather arrives. This foresight eliminates much of the frustration that can arise due to broken, worn, or poorly maintained gear. Sweeping out your portable ice shanty and carefully examining the exterior for any tears, holes, or excess weathering is much easier to accomplish outdoors in the fall than in the first 20-below cold snap. Checking spark plugs, fuel, and the blades on an auger guarantees fishing will actually take place. Cleaning and lubricating fishing reels and tip-ups, then adding some fresh line, is much easier inside a warm house or garage than on the ice. Tying on jigs and bobber stops before reaching your destination ensures warm fingers for a longer period of time—plus less chance of making a mistake.

CHAPTER THREE

Ice Electronics

Talking about electronics for your boat might not seem to make sense when visiting the topic of ice fishing, but it does. Purchasing a single sonar unit that can function effectively both on the ice and in the boat will save a nice chunk of money. And *that* should make sense to every angler.

Flasher Sonar

Because of its popularity and effectiveness, flasher sonar is owned and used by many ice anglers. Encountering other anglers nearby that are using the same or similarly operating flashers is one of the potential difficulties in using the units. Many of today's flashers operate at or around 200 kHz. If another unit is nearby emitting sound signals into the water, a neighboring unit can sometimes receive some of the sound, which interferes with that unit's own cycle of sending and receiving sound signals.

Interference can be a problem not just on open ice, but inside a fish house. Angling generally being a social endeavor, especially when it comes to ice fishing, it's quite common to have several anglers inside a large fish house, each using their own hole hoping to land a whopper. If a handful of the occupants are utilizing sonar to keep an eye on their bait and watch for approaching fish, the sound signals emitted and received underwater jumble, causing interference on the electronic displays.

Any marine electronics unit with a transducer close to 200 kHz can experience and contribute to interference. The transducer sends sound signals, audibly recognized as clicks or ticks, into the water. These sounds are produced at a certain rate, with the same consistency of a ticking clock, but much faster. The transducer then receives the return signal once the sound has bounced off the bottom or, even better, a fish. If that transducer is interpreting the return signal and simultaneously picks up a signal from another unit, this instantly affects accuracy, and the display shows targets that are not really present.

Unfortunately, the transducer's emitted sound is not simply contained within a finite vertical plane; it "bleeds" into the water and can easily affect other flashers in the immediate vicinity. However, there is a solution. Many flashers, including those made by Vexilar, now have an interference rejection feature that allows the operator to change the rate and pitch of the sound emitted from the transducer so it does not coincide with another person's electronics. This enables a group of friends to fish within the confines of an ice house without having the functionality of their electronics compromised. One particular model of flasher, the Vexilar FL-20, has twelve different interference rejection modes, giving you plenty of opportunity to change the signal coming from your electronics.

The interference rejection feature changes the pulse of sound produced by the transducer, making it more difficult for other units to misinterpret the signal. Unfortunately, sound released into the water does not necessarily travel in a prescribed direction. Instead, the signal "bleeds" in all directions. Fortunately, by using the interference rejection system, each angler in the fish house can change his or her rate and pitch of the transducer's audible signal to provide an accurate display.

Another highly influential attribute of your transducer is the cone angle. This relates to the area your flasher can effectively "see." Vexilar offers transducers from a narrow 9-degree option, to the standard 12-degree component, ending at the wide 19-degree viewing angle. You can also get a combination transducer that has both 9-degree and 19-degree capabilities housed within one transducer body.

The narrow 9-degree and wide 19-degree viewing angles provide increased flexibility via an easily accessible switch allowing alternation between the two.

So what's the advantage to having narrow and wide-angled transducers? A narrow-beam transducer works great when you need less clutter on your screen, like when you're trying to determine fish present in tall weeds. A wide-angle transducer in that situation displays more clutter, showing more weeds that make it harder to decipher fish mixed in between the vegetation. The wide-angle transducer is best in deeper water to see apprehensive fish circling your bait from afar. The narrow-beam transducer is great in moderate to heavy vegetation because the cone has a smaller viewing area, displaying fewer obstructions in the process.

A flasher or any type of sonar covers an area dependent upon the cone angle of the accompanying transducer. If utilizing a transducer with a 12-degree cone angle, you will see an area approximately one-fifth of the depth you're fishing. For instance, a 12-degree transducer in 30 feet of water will display an area that's about 6 feet wide. With a 19-degree transducer, you'll see an area about one-third of your current depth, which in 30 feet of water would be an approximate 10-foot diameter of "visible" water.

With any transducer, it is important to keep it level as it projects sound pulses down your ice hole. Vexilar flashers have an innovative Ice-Ducer that integrates a foam

■ Flasher sonar units and ice fishing go hand-in-hand. Without the aid of the flasher to relay important information such as depth, bottom type, weed availability, and fish presence, the angler can only blindly assume what's taking place below the ice.

float with the cable, allowing it to suspend directly beneath the float because of gravitational pull. There are no leveling bubbles needed, just good old-fashioned physics.

As stated previously, one of the greatest attributes of a flasher is that it not only shows fish waiting below, but it also enables the angler to recognize when there aren't any fish below, which indicates the need to change either presentation or location.

Sometimes when you drop the transducer into a new hole, a fish (or at least what seems to be one) appears a few feet off the bottom but never moves or bites. This could be interference if another angler is fishing nearby, which is easily eliminated using your unit's interference rejection. However, it is more likely that the object you are seeing is the top of a weed stalk or a branch. You may not even hook the object with effort, but remember that even in relatively shallow water you will see an area large enough to accommodate the angled protrusion while your bait rises and falls without making contact. Try fishing both above and below the target, and if nothing else comes in after a short period and the object doesn't change depth, move on.

Even though the Vexilar flasher cannot identify the precise species, it does show their mannerisms, which can often translate into a presumption of a particular type of fish. For instance, northern pike show up as a thick signal but have fast, intermittent flashes due to the pulsating of their fins and gills. They appear and dis-

appear quickly and sometimes move vertically with great speed. If you want positive identification for the species, position an Aqua-Vu underwater camera (see the Underwater Cameras section) in another hole close by. It's like watching the fish on television, and the black-and-white image leaves no doubt as to what you're chasing. You can even record the encounter digitally using the digital video recording accessory (DVR).

Underwater Cameras

Upon introduction, underwater cameras were ten times the cost of today. Anglers can now purchase a basic underwater camera kit for $100, though prices increase for models of higher quality with additional options including lighting type (infrared or spectral response); on-screen display of camera depth, temperature, and direction; screen style (cathode-ray tube or liquid crystal display); cable length; and monitor size. Some systems employ multiple cameras for 360-degree viewing capacity, a worthy, yet cost-escalating option.

Generally, an underwater camera will see approximately double the distance visible by the naked human eye, meaning water clarity of 4 feet would offer about 8 feet of viewable distance. Available light dynamically affects the equation, an issue during operation at dusk and in deep water.

Deploying a camera into the same hole you're fishing through provides close perspective but additionally creates

FLASHER MALFUNCTION

There are a few simple steps to identify malfunction issues arising with any flasher. The majority of equipment failures involve the power supply. Check the connections to the battery to make sure that they are secure and clean, and then confirm a well-charged battery. You can alleviate most problems by ensuring a fully charged and functional battery.

If the battery is working correctly, check the transducer. Frequent vibration, impact, or scratches on the face of the transducer can negatively impact its performance. If the outer covering of the transducer cable is sliced, repair it with a waterproof tape, but a severed internal wire requires delivery to customer service or an entirely new transducer before your flasher will function properly.

Pat Aschoff, a Vexilar service technician, offers some insight regarding flasher repair. "Individuals have different levels of skill. As a service tech at Vexilar, I would never tell a customer they could fix their own unit or transducer cord. You cannot believe (or maybe you can) how many units I receive to be repaired because someone thought they could 'fix it themselves.' Instead, simply send the unit to the Vexilar Service Department for repair. If a customer works on the unit, the cost for me to repair it is typically more than the original repair might have cost, since attempted self-repair often causes additional damage. It's really best to stay out of the unit. Shipping the flasher to customer service will save you money in the long run."

■ Dragging your transducer from hole to hole decreases the life of the fragile barium titanate crystal housed inside. Avoiding this practice will save you money, as a damaged transducer is typically irreparable, and replacement becomes mandatory to accurate functioning.

an obstacle. Navigating around the camera cable while battling a fish is difficult, often resulting in a tangled mess and a hot temper. In addition, the macro view of your bait prohibits a larger view of the perimeter. By placing the camera farther away, a larger area around your bait is visible. Yet if the water clarity is limited, a position near the hook is the only possible option.

To remedy the issue of entanglement with the camera cable, drill an additional hole a few inches to a few feet away from your primary fishing hole and drop the camera down. This extra distance acts as a buffer, although the fierce run of a pike, hefty largemouth bass, or any other fish of substantial size may still cause the cable and fishing line to intertwine.

The distance you choose for spacing the angling and viewing holes depends upon water clarity. Crystal-clear water allows a greater distance between holes, while dirtier water requires less distance. In clear-water environments, a properly positioned camera can monitor the activity of multiple lines.

Sonar vs. Underwater Cameras

With the introduction of underwater viewing units, some anglers attempt to compare sonar with underwater cameras. In all honesty, they are two separate entities. Both use innovative technology in their creation, but when it comes down to application, sonar is greatly advantageous while angling. With sonar, there are no cameras to deploy or cords to hold. Both hands are free to hold rods, tie knots, and fight fish, and an angler can see the Vexilar super-bright displays from several feet away, even in bright sunlight.

Cameras are indeed beneficial for effectively understanding the underwater environment, which can ultimately earn you more fish. They offer a positive identification of fish species and weed classes, a valuable asset after finding the targets using a flasher. Yet an underwater camera has a number of variables that influence its efficiency, the most dramatic being water clarity. Water clarity has very little effect on the display of a flasher, but stained water quickly diminishes the visual field of a camera. Floating sediment is another Achilles heel of an underwater camera, and an abundance of suspended particles creates great difficulties. Cameras equipped with infrared or spectral response lights don't remedy the situation. In fact, engaging the factory-equipped lighting source creates a "snowstorm effect," further diminishing the visual field.

If you can afford a flasher and an underwater camera, you will possess two valuable tools. It's always interesting to drop a camera down on a school of fish seen on the flasher, only to discover they are not the previously assumed, or desired, species.

An underwater camera is a valuable asset in relatively clear water, but positioning the lens to view your bait takes some patience and expertise. Finding a hook within close proximity of the bottom involves gently twisting the cable to rotate the camera. Once your bait is visible on the display, simply hook the cable on a "keeper." Some cameras have a notch on the housing to provide a secure place to hook the cable, eliminating the need to hold it in your hand. Yet periodic adjustment to the camera angle is often necessary.

Another option is to purchase an underwater stand. These attach to the actual camera and, once dropped down the hole, keep the camera upright. The concept has some merit, but the function depends upon too many variables. If there is any weed cover, the camera sits within the vegetation. A soft bottom causes the stand to angle, sink into the muck, or fall over.

A better solution is an Aqua-Vu Mod-Pod or similar above-water tripod. The Mod-Pod permits easy viewing by integrating a motor into a tripod stand positioned directly above the ice hole. A remote control operates the mechanism, giving the angler ultimate control. Non-motorized stands are an alternative, but performing adjustments requires a pause in the fishing action.

Sonar vs. Sonar

Assuming that the electronics mounted on your boat, with a few modifications, can function properly on the ice will only disappoint the user. Though a liquid crystal graph might offer outstanding performance under open-water conditions, ice fishing presents numerous obstacles.

First and foremost, extreme cold can slow down conventional LCD sonar or stop it altogether. Since accurate response is one of the greatest attributes of sonar, this already presents a disadvantage. Simple considerations, such as the material used to construct the selection buttons and knobs, aren't as stringent for blue-water compared to ice fishing. If even one small component of the sonar fails, it can have a detrimental effect on the entire unit.

Conversely, electronics used during winter *can* cross over to the boat. Flasher design, for instance, effectively conforms beyond winter's unilateral application. Their effectiveness in the boat rivals their performance on the ice.

Vexilar's Pro Packs and Ultra Packs are quite popular and come with everything needed to fish on the ice. Having the ability to grab one of the packages from the shelf and use it immediately is quite convenient. Yet tossing the ever-popular Ice-Ducer over the side of the boat will not provide the same detail as it does on ice. Since the Styrofoam float gently rocks between the crest and trough of waves, the transducer follows, inconsistently projecting sound in an undesirable pattern. The floating transducer might also hit or rub against the boat, possibly causing damage to the transducer or watercraft. A better solution is either a high-speed transducer designed for the transom of the boat, or a

■ Although bluegill are one of the smallest varieties of targeted freshwater fish through the ice, they're not small enough to escape the watchful eye of a flasher or underwater camera.

puck-style transducer that attaches to the underside of a trolling motor, available in special conversion kits. Either option greatly improves the unit's performance in the boat. In addition, when the ice arrives once again, you can simply remove the unit from the gimbaled bracket on the boat and mount it in your ice fishing electronics carrying case. The process only takes a few minutes and doesn't require any tools.

The Three, Two, One Approach

Maximizing one's ability to catch fish is a prime reason anglers continually refine their techniques, gathering input from others, reading about fishing, keeping logs with pertinent information—all to, plain and simply, help them catch more fish. On the ice, the Three, Two, One approach is any easy way to increase catch rates for practically any species. The basic idea entails three holes, two ice fishing rods, and one flasher.

In states where more than one line is legal per individual angler, pairing two ice fishing rods and reels with different presentations allows the angler more flexibility to discover the preferred technique by winter fish of any species. Flasher owners have the unique ability of pulling double duty with their electronics, utilizing their unit to see activity in two separate holes. Drilling three holes in a line with only a few inches between them allows transducer placement in the center hole, displaying the two separate baits dropped down simultaneously in the two outer holes. If the water is shallow, the hole positions must be very close to one another and may not clearly show both baits, but as you move into deeper water, the transducer can see increasingly larger areas. The standard transducer angle for a Vexilar flasher is 12 degrees, which means in 10 feet of water you can see an area approximately 2.2 feet wide. However,

■ Where permissible, simultaneously using multiple rods increases your chances of catching fish. Strategically drilling a third hole between two active lines creates the ideal spot for placing your flasher transducer and protects it from entanglement when battling fish.

this is the distance you would see if your gain was turned to the maximum, which it is not when you're fishing, so the actual area is slightly less. In 20 feet of water an angler can see approximately 4.3 feet, and in 30 feet about 6.3 feet. So in theory you could place the outer two holes of your three-hole sequence over 6 feet apart if you're fishing in 30 feet. Well, that would be overly simplified, and there would certainly be some difficulties, especially when trying to jig with a rod in each hand with holes placed that far apart—you'd be better off using long, open-water rods instead of ice fishing sticks! And the fish would have to be located right on the bottom to fall within the zone of where the transducer could actually "see," while suspended fish may go unnoticed past the narrower portion of the transducer's cone. Getting back to reality, spacing the holes about 6 inches apart from one another in 10 feet and 16 inches apart in 20 feet works well assuming you're using an 8-inch auger. And because the transducer is secluded in the privacy of the middle hole, you don't have to pull up

the transducer cable when you latch into a big fish.

A popular add-on to the Vexilar flashers is the LED FlexLight, which is a welcome addition when fishing very early in the morning or into the night. Since the FlexLight consists of three super-bright LEDs, the energy draw is measured in milliamps, a fraction of what conventional light sources use for energy and only one-tenth the power your flasher requires. In fact, the FlexLight uses only 25 milliamps, meaning you can run it continuously with Vexilar's 9-amp battery for twelve days straight! When used in conjunction with your Vexilar flasher, the two can operate for about twenty-five hours on a fully charged battery, giving you plenty of time to catch a big one. And for anglers who want to use the three-hole, two-rod, one-flasher technique, two FlexLights can be mounted to the Pro Packs and Ultra Packs, giving you illumination for both of the prime outer fishing holes. Begin your countdown for more fish now—Three, Two, One . . .

CHAPTER FOUR

Ice Fishing through the Season

Just as the open-water season divides into different periods, such as spring, pre-spawn, spawn, post-spawn, early summer, late summer, fall, etc., ice fishing also segments, though not as diversely. Early ice, midwinter, and late ice are three periods to consider.

Early Ice

The early ice period begins with the first skims of ice and can be one of the most dangerous times to fish. Three inches of ice is an acceptable depth to begin walking safely, given the thickness is consistent. It's quite common to find 3 inches of ice near the shoreline and much less only a few steps out. Other factors can also contribute to inconsistency of ice thickness. Current, springs, seeping water, wind, depth of water, even the presence of large schools of fish can affect ice formation. It's difficult to visually discriminate variations in ice thickness without chiseling or drilling a hole, and with snow cover it's impossible, so be very careful during the first expeditions of the year. Waiting one more week or at least a few more days to ensure your safety could save your life. In other words, think realistically.

The early ice period is usually one of rapid activity. A newly enclosed underwater world confines the fish, and both excitement and apprehension are evident. Metabolic rates drop, and even though fish may be active, it's much different behavior compared to open-water activity. Some fish will go days, weeks, even months without eating or adversely expending energy to chase a meal, while others aggressively wander in search of sustenance. This behavior does not relegate to one species, location, or time of day. Baits much smaller than those used during the open-water months are required, and the fish make very few exceptions. Crankbaits have no use. Neither do spinnerbaits. Nearly all baits cast and retrieved on a semihorizontal plane remain ineffective because of the vertical presentation required by the ice angler's position.

Midwinter

After the ice has gained depth and snow has accumulated on the surface, the weather

■ The snow-free glaze over the lake at first ice requires caution. Otherwise, thin ice and a slippery surface can lead to injury.
BILL LINDNER

typically cools more each day, and as January and February approach, sub-zero temperatures are the norm rather than the exception. This midwinter period is one of unpredictability. The presence of fish remains important when determining a productive area, but fish attitude plays a huge role. Extreme cold can cause fish activity to plummet and seriously affects the angler's ability to remain mobile. Drilling a series of holes, sometimes turning an entire bay into a landscape that looks more like Swiss cheese, now becomes a major feat. Nimble fingers quickly numb even under the heaviest covering, and augers that once spun smoothly now chortle and whine under the tension of cold. Holes freeze over fast, and fish intended to be released have less time to make it in before their fins get freezer burn, sometimes fatally so. Yet the midwinter period typically produces some of the biggest fish of the entire year, open water included. Many of the larger gamefish have already started developing eggs for spawning in the spring and subsist on high-calorie diets that in turn provide greater girth. This pattern of indiscriminate feeding caters to ice anglers, and although the overall population of fish in general may seem sluggish at times, windows of activity provide some great angling action.

Late Ice

The late ice period is one of renewed activity. As the snowpack begins to melt, a definite transition begins. Fish search for food to further develop size and gain energy to reproduce, whereas the majority of winter is spent eating simply to survive.

Some areas of the Midwest begin closing seasons for some gamefish to protect them as they approach spawning. For instance, walleye, bass, muskie, and northern pike seasons in Minnesota close the second Sunday in February. Of those four species, muskies spawn first, in mid- to late April, and then northern pike immediately follow, commonly overlapping with the muskies. Walleye are the next to spawn, laying their eggs in early May. Largemouth bass reproduce in late May, and smallmouth bass follow up in early June. Looking at the calendar, open season for those species closes noticeably earlier than their actual spawning date, but these fish remain protected for this period due to their susceptibility.

All species of fish, protected or not, become increasingly active during the late ice period. Melting snow seeps into open ice holes, flushing food particles into the lakes while creating numerous, small currents that attract panfish, with larger gamefish preying on the panfish. This textbook example of the food chain can be witnessed beneath a single ice hole.

The late ice period can also be a dangerous time for anglers. Thick ice that once supported large trucks and dark houses thins quickly. Weekend warriors discover dramatic transformations after a handful of days, which can be hazardous if one is not cautious. At some point late in the season, the snow completely disappears, and a gas auger can whip the operator in circles if he or she isn't wearing slip-on ice cleats. Life jackets and throw ropes are cautionary gear suggestions, and trekking with a partner is a must.

Getting out to good ice during the late ice period can be an adventure in itself. Areas of the lake that receive less direct sunlight throughout the course of the day obviously have the greatest potential for allowing easy access to strong ice. Although sunlight direction plays an active role in melting the ice, obstructions like trees and hillsides can block ice-deteriorating sunlight.

A long wood plank can function as a boardwalk once the ice separates a few feet from the shoreline. However, catching late-ice fish of any species isn't worth the price of your life. Carefully weigh the odds before attempting a late-season ice fishing trip.

■ The late ice period is met with longer days and more direct sunlight, enjoyed by anglers as they shed their coats for sweatshirts and, at times, only a T-shirt.

IF YOU'RE ON THIN ICE. . .

The Minnesota Department of Natural Resources makes these safety recommendations in case the unthinkable happens.

What if a companion falls through thin ice?

- Keep calm and think out a solution.

- Don't run up to the hole. You'll probably break through and then there will be two victims.

- Use some item on shore to throw or extend to the victim to pull them out of the water, such as jumper cables or skis, or push a boat ahead of you.

- If you can't rescue the victim immediately, call 911. It's amazing how many people carry cell phones.

- Get medical assistance for the victim. People who are subjected to cold water immersion but seem fine after being rescued can suffer a potentially fatal condition called "after drop," which may occur when cold blood that is pooled in the body's extremities starts to circulate again as the victim starts to re-warm.

What if YOU fall in?

- Try not to panic. Instead, remain calm and turn toward the direction you came from. Place your hands and arms on the unbroken surface of the ice (here's where ice picks come in handy). Work forward on the ice by kicking your feet. If the ice breaks, maintain your position and slide forward again. Once you are lying on the ice, don't stand. Instead, roll away from the hole. That spreads out your weight until you are on solid ice. This sounds much easier than it really is to do.

- The best advice is don't put yourself into needless danger by venturing out too soon or too late in the season. No angler, no matter how much of a fishing enthusiast, would want to die for a crappie.

©2008 Minnesota Department of Natural Resources. Used with permission.

Safety through the Season

Even at its thickest development, ice is never entirely safe. Any type of water movement, stress from expansion or weight, and deterioration from sunlight and sediment deposits all affect the integrity of ice. Current from inlets and outlets, and moving water from schools of fish or fluctuating water levels can affect ice thickness and strength.

Sand and salt left on the lake from vehicles recently traveling down maintained highways and gravel access roads can accumulate over the course of the winter, causing minimal damage to the ice—until late in the season. The tiny rocks and salt granules permeate the ice quickly once heated by the sun's rays.

Late in the season, emergent weeds such as pencil reeds and bulrushes act as vertical solar panels, heating the general vicinity more rapidly compared to wide-open, mid-lake regions. During this period, fishing equipment lying on the ice gradually warms and slowly melts the ice beneath. For instance, leaving an ice chisel or scoop on the ice for an hour produces an identical outline in the ice, a temporary fossil of your late-season outing. Debris from other anglers melts through the ice in a similar manner. This can cause hazardous ice conditions for anglers if they are not acutely aware of their surroundings.

It's perfectly normal for ice to groan, crack, and gurgle as the water freezes and expands, but warming ice also "talks." In some cases the sounds are relatively harmless, but as spring approaches and the ice becomes thin, these sounds can indicate danger. If the ice gets extremely "vocal," it's better to leave.

Ice heaves, otherwise known as pressure ridges, are very dangerous, and anglers should avoid them whenever possible. Driving a vehicle, ATV, or snowmobile or even walking near an ice heave can break it, potentially causing the ice angler to fall into the chilly water. Even if the angler avoids drowning by successfully climbing out of the lake, hypothermia becomes a dangerous issue. As a general rule, larger bodies of water have a greater likelihood of producing pressure ridges, but the possibility exists on small lakes, too.

Ropes, picks, life jackets, and even that five-gallon bucket can be lifesavers when navigating open ice, especially unfamiliar areas. No ice is ever completely safe, and caution is the best remedy for getting wet.

Winter Fish Care

Once out on the lake, it's every angler's intention to land some fish. Whether or not you keep any is a personal choice, but take extreme care when releasing fish back into their underwater environment.

When fishing open ice, extremely cold temperatures can be fatal to any species of fish when hauled out of the water. Fins, gills, and eyes can quickly freeze once exposed to below-freezing winds. Ambient temperatures that plunge below zero permit a limited window of time for keeping fish out of the water. In certain conditions, this can be less than a minute.

Sliding large gamefish out of the ice hole onto the ice can harm the fish if it's recklessly flopped on jagged ice crystals, scraping its scales and protective slime, which can increase the possibility of future infection.

Grabbing a fish while wearing cloth gloves can also remove some of its protective slime. Ideally, the angler should wet bare hands beforehand, but we all know how difficult that can be in sub-zero situations.

■ Releasing fish permits future reproduction. However, carefully consider the health of the fish before letting it go, as a deeply hooked fish may not survive.
CHIP LEER

Taking refuge in a fish house can protect your hands, but does not always protect the fish. Keeping fish out of water for extended periods can be detrimental to their health. A good reference point is to hold your breath once landing a fish, and then attempt to release it before you run out of air. For most people this allows less than a minute to grab the fish, take out the hook, snap a quick picture, and throw it back.

Modern fish houses often have carpeted floors, and the stiff, all-weather flooring can seriously hurt a fish that writhes and flops on the surface. Anglers should make a concerted effort to prevent fish from coming into contact with the abrasive covering.

Keeping Live Bait Lively

Staying warm in sub-zero conditions is hard enough, but keeping your bait from freezing is another challenge in itself. Larvae tend to turn into miniature ice cubes when their container is left sitting on the

■ Is it a mouse or a worm? Mousies are one variety of larva that panfish of all varieties rarely resist. Trading the thin plastic tub for an insulated container prevents a quick-freeze when exposed to the elements. The inside pocket of a fishing parka keeps the worms in a warm environment, close to your body.

ice or sometimes even the fish house floor. Few anglers enjoy warming frozen larvae between their cheek and gum. Keeping the worm container in your pocket protects the bait longer, but placing it inside an interior pocket situates the bait closer to your body, warming it and preventing the chance for freezing.

Typically, tackle shops sell waxworms, maggots, eurolarve, mousies, spikes, and mealworms in small deli-style containers holding a few dozen or in larger plastic containers housing hundreds of critters. Trading the flimsy container for a stronger, insulated case delays freezing, but does not guarantee ice-free bait.

Lindy's Grub-Getter is a nice container for worms due to a perforated divider that separates worms from sawdust or bedding, making it easy to grab a worm quickly, an asset when trying to get your fingers back into your gloves!

Minnows are another issue entirely. Keeping a bucket of minnows tight to your body inside your jacket isn't possible. Even Styrofoam-insulated buckets eventually freeze in arctic temperatures. One idea is to use a floating live well for minnows. These cylindrical nets fit perfectly inside an ice hole while a foam ring keeps the contraption afloat. Dumping your minnow supply inside the live well keeps them invigorated without freezing. When it's time to leave the lake, scoop some water into a five-gallon bucket and transport the fish back home.

Leaving minnows in the vehicle overnight results in a frozen mass of dead bait, yet keeping the minnow pail in the basement until the next weekend rarely works out unless you properly care for your small finned friends. If the water begins to diminish in quality, replace it using well water, as municipal water treatments will kill live bait. Oxygenating the water is another preventive measure and keeps minnows alive longer. Small battery-operated aerators are available for under $10 and are worth ten times their price.

Finally, remove dead minnows from your bucket immediately. Decomposition requires oxygen and also contaminates the water. Stated simply: clean water and oxygen will keep your minnows alive until the next trip.

CHAPTER FIVE

Ice-Time Walleye

Walleye, generally considered the best-tasting freshwater fish available, are a popular target for ice anglers. People regularly catch "ol' marble eyes" throughout the day during winter due to elongated periods of low light that walleye prefer. Ambient light diminishes greatly underwater, even on relatively clear lakes, but a sheet of ice and several inches of snow further reduce the available light. Walleye have exceptional sight and prefer low-light periods, so ice fishing actually caters to their preference.

Traditional fall hot spots are viable starting locations for winter walleye. Lake maps are an inexpensive source for locating potential fish structure such as steep drop-offs, rock, sand and rubble substrates, as well as points, humps, and saddles, all classic habitat for walleye. The advent of electronics, especially flashers with real-time displays and portable GPS units (covered in chapters two and three), makes locating walleye through the ice much easier than what our ancestors experienced.

Locating Early-Ice Walleyes

The itch can keep you up at night. Waiting out the period of time when bodies of water first freeze until there's safe walking ice is a killer. Pure agony. Yet trying to "will" good ice won't keep you safe. I would not recommend sliding across the ice on a 4 x 8-foot sheet of plywood to redistribute your weight-to-area ratio.

Why the impatience? Early ice typically produces some great action. Even though fish are adapting to a recently changed environment, with water that has mixed, eliminating stratification, their feeding mood is often positive, despite the overhead canopy of ice. Snow cover reduces sunlight penetration, making vision and weed growth more difficult, yet the sudden, drastic transformation after the first snowfall doesn't seem to affect the fish adversely.

Because the first ice fishing trips of the season often take place while the ice is relatively thin, at least comparatively to the 30 inches encountered at the height of the year, location and mobility must be carefully considered. Hiking several miles across the lake doesn't sound appealing with an auger, portable fish house, electronics, rods, reels, and a heater in tow. It doesn't take much time, maybe a week or two, for the ice to grow thick enough to support an ATV or snowmobile once you've already been traveling on the encased water by foot.

Early-season walleye often mirror the locations held during the latest part of fall. Many anglers put their boats in storage once the leaves begin to drop, but those engaging in cold-water fishing exploits experience some of the best fishing of the year while gathering clues for locating walleye once the ice arrives. Easy access to logical walleye hot spots can be difficult if the entire lake, due to sheer size, isn't manageable by foot. Yet there are definitely hot spots near your entry point that will put a bend in your rod.

The equation for productive fishing sounds simple: First find the fish, then get them to bite. Unfortunately for anglers, numerous variables underlie those two tenets. Understanding fish location as your first priority creates a practical procedure for beginning your winter walleye quest.

Each lake differs dramatically, and fish location is equally diverse. No single formula leads an angler to the fish every time on every lake. Walleye are no different, but understanding their positional preferences eliminates much of the guesswork.

Their fondness for certain substrates and variegated topography provides some general guidelines when selecting areas to fish. Rock, gravel, and sand bottoms remain most attractive to walleye. Pair this with a defining structural element such as a hump, deepwater bar, or steep drop-off, and you have the potential for walleye presence.

Early-ice walleye action is fast. The fish are hungry, and access to their position is easy without loads of travel-prohibiting snow. Larger presentations in medial depths attract early-season walleye and entertain anglers as they capitalize on the first peak of ice fishing activity.

Begin your early-ice outing by exploring points, bars, and shoreline drop-offs. Primary drops that descend to 15 to 20 feet are good areas to start since their bases offer pathways for both fish and forage to follow. Shallower depths, although potentially catering to the occasional wandering walleye, don't suit the natural desires held by larger groups of fish. Access to deep water is an important attribute for walleye location, offering both forage and refuge at certain times. As baitfish wander the natural bottom contours, walleye trail in hot pursuit.

Anglers have also discovered the common draw of deep, weed-line edges for early-ice walleye. Though known for their attraction to hard bottoms, walleye find solace in the cover of vegetation, ambushing prey from within the weed stalks.

Spot-on-the-spot areas lend variety for early-season 'eyes. An isolated weed clump on the peak of a mid-range bar or

■ Walleye are a wildly popular species for ice anglers. Lakes with a strong forage base provide the best opportunity for catching beauties like this. CHIP LEER

small rock pile seated adjacent to the outer perimeter of a weed line are subtle abnormalities that walleye love. Finding these minor differences in structure are important when looking for fish.

Midwinter Walleye

Temperatures dive. Snow cover accumulates. Walleye move deeper. Anglers seeking out midwinter walleye should start their day on the outer perimeter of structure. Shallow-water regions remain fruitless for the most part as oxygen levels drop in accord with decomposing vegetation. Main-lake, deepwater components like humps, reefs, deep bars, and small basin areas are most attractive to walleye following the turn of a new calendar year. During this period, protruding bottom structure like humps and reefs are best if they peak in the 15- to 20-foot range with deep water along the outer perimeter. Walleye often travel atop the crest of these humps and subsequently explore the edges, moving toward secondary drops as dictated by the presence of forage. These deepwater havens possess consistency in temperature and a better food supply as compared to the early-season, shallower locales.

Structure located outside the range where first-ice walleye once roamed promotes inhabitance. A small rise of the bottom along a deepwater flat, a handful of large boulders beyond the base of a primary drop-off, or several stalks of green vegetation slightly deeper and offset from an otherwise weedless hump give midwinter walleye a point of reference for establishment.

Deep, soft-bottomed basins also attract walleye as they migrate in search of forage, which becomes increasingly hard to find as winter progresses. Slight differences in bottom type promote the existence of wandering walleye in these instances. Mud substrates that quickly transition to another bottom type, such as gravel or sand, allow walleye to access forage relating to two differing elements.

One important factor to consider when making a run at deeper, midwinter walleye is light. During most times of the year, walleye prefer feeding during low-light periods, specifically near dawn and dusk. Utilizing brightly colored jigs and lures promotes their detection by walleye under low-light conditions. Luminescent baits are another popular addition to the ice fishing arsenal, especially for walleye. Their subtle, colorful haze allows walleye to easily locate your presentation from a distance before sunrise and at dusk. In midwinter, deepwater zones present similar situations. As light penetration lessens in correlation with increases in depth, visual acuity diminishes, giving reason for anglers to use bright-colored or glow presentations no matter the time of day.

Late-Winter Walleye

Many ice anglers aren't able to chase walleye late into the year, primarily due to the closure of their season. Most regions where ice fishing takes place prohibit walleye harvest during March and April because of their susceptibility as they embark on a ravenous feeding foray, packing in the necessary nutrients for reproductive development. Egg-laden walleye remain positioned near their midwinter haunts until the ice has almost entirely decomposed, at which point the fish begin moving toward staging areas before the spawn.

Walleye Presentation and Technique

Getting walleye to bite through the ice is much different compared to open-water techniques. There is no trolling. There is no casting. A vertical plane confines your presentation's motion, unless the lure's action provides a wider range achieved by darting and swimming.

Bait, Dead or Alive

Live bait is a common choice for anglers wanting to catch winter walleye, but nightcrawlers and leeches are a bust. Minnows, specifically shiners and fatheads, are the primary live-bait choice, although other minnow varieties and waxworks on certain lures work all right, too. If opting for live bait, it should be just that—alive. Wiggling tails, undulating fins, and flaring gills are important features when attempting to gain a walleye's attention.

Fresh dead bait is another good choice if configured correctly. An entire dead minnow hanging lifeless from a stationary jig will not produce many fish. Nevertheless, a portion of fresh dead bait, like the head of a fathead pinched off, not cut, hooked on the end of a jigging spoon combines the action of live or injured prey with a strong scent trail because of the fresh dead bait. Why not simply dead bait? Yes, fresh dead bait does sound like an oxymoron, but take the same situation and apply it to human preference. Would you rather eat freshly caught fish, going straight to the kitchen from the lake, or fillets that had been lying around for a while? Even though fish may not detect culinary discrepancies like humans, they do have preferences.

Scoop Up Walleye with Jigging Spoons

Smaller versions of baits used during the summer work best for most species during winter, yet there are some seasonally specific baits that work very well and should be an integral part of your winter walleye plan. One is the jigging spoon. Although jigging spoons are capable of producing some great open-water walleye catches, they aren't commonplace. During winter, they are a walleye angler's staple. Various weights, colors, sizes, and designs of jigging spoons are mandatory in every ice fishing tackle box.

The first spoon to consider is Lindy's Rattl'r spoon. It's a densely weighted spoon that carries a brass rattle on its back, producing an audible clamor when

■ Walleye can easily see the flash of a jigging spoon from great distances. Although spoons work under nearly any condition, certain situations, such as shallow water, low-light periods, and diminished water clarity, are ideal circumstances for spoon-feeding walleye.

put into motion. Another Lindy design is the Frostee spoon, a wider, but thinner spoon with a luminescent paint finish called Techni-Glo that glows brightly when charged with the Lindy Tazer. The Tazer is essentially a concentrated flashlight. Its small size allows you to put it in your pocket or tackle box, or clip it to your zipper. The concentrated beam of light quickly "charges" the finish to a bright glow that can be seen from afar in low-light conditions. The Tazer works on any type of glow-in-the-dark paint.

The third jigging spoon produced by Lindy that is a fabulous walleye attractor is the Flyer jigging spoon. This bait has a flared head, which prompts the bait to flick, flip, and fly through the water, provoking attention from all species of fish, especially walleye. Its internal rattle helps fish locate its position in low-visibility situations, and the finish looks highly appealing.

Tipping the spoons with live or artificial baits is standard protocol when fishing for walleye. A pinched-off minnow head usually does the trick, or an entire lively minnow of a smaller variety hooked carefully through the lips is another option. Artificial alternatives include Berkley's Gulp! and Powerbait products as well as Lindy's Munchies Tiny Tails. The Berkley Gulp! puts out 400 times more scent in the water compared to traditional plastic baits and is biodegradable. Fish love it, but you can't simple hang a Gulp! frog from the treble hook of a jigging spoon and expect to catch walleye. The Gulp! maggots are an ideal choice—or simply cut a small chunk from a larger bait to put on the hook. You can cut off the head of one of the Gulp! minnows to give it a natural appearance and scent, or simply go the scent route and hack off a small nugget from virtually any Gulp! product, even the frog, as long as you don't use it in its entirety.

So why go with artificial bait instead of live bait? First, artificial bait cannot die since it was never alive. There is less time spent changing bait or getting a fresh minnow, which equates to longer periods of time with your hands in your gloves. Your *warm* gloves. Artificial bait is easy to transport—no cumbersome pails accompanied by the weight of water—and artificial bait can be used where live bait, due to restrictions, cannot. Hike-in and fly-in trips often prohibit the use of live bait, therefore making artificial attractors your only, yet extremely productive, option.

Jigging Spoon Techniques

Simply tying on a jigging spoon doesn't automatically guarantee walleye, especially when it comes to pressured fisheries and super-clear underwater environments that allow walleye to scrutinize any presentation.

A good jigging spoon becomes even better when the proper technique is used. Yet determining what constitutes *proper* is an ongoing compendium of trial and error to decipher what triggers a positive response from the fish. Even a spoon with a mediocre appearance can become a reliable strike producer if combined with the right technique.

Selecting a spoon based upon technique is a good start. For instance, if ripping the spoon with erratic, sweeping motions of the rod, a spoon with a slightly bent body will veer and fall at an angle. The Lindy Flyer jigging spoon does a complete somersault at its topmost ascent, while the Lindy Rattl'r spoon descends in varying directions. Conversely, the Lindy Frostee jigging spoon has a design that provides less horizontal motion. This proves productive when shaking the spoon or when "A-bombing" the bottom as an attractor.

Slick Spoons for Tricky Walleye— Invigorating Response from Fickle Fish

Jigging spoons are a staple in any adept walleye angler's ice fishing tackle arsenal. Size, shape, color, action, profile, and auditory production are attributes that have an effect on the likability of a spoon. Some jigging spoons simply don't seem to catch fish, while others turn weary walleye passionately enthusiastic.

Spoons are performing aerial acrobats, producing breathtaking flips, turns, and lightning-fast descents that command attention. Such activity is hard for walleye to resist no matter what type of lake you're fishing. Spoon-feeding presentations are great for clear-water situations because hungry walleye can see the bait's erratic dancing from great distances, luring them to close proximity from afar. This is extremely beneficial since ice fishing entails luring fish nearer to your position. Coaxing, coercing, and convincing walleye to approach a bait is necessary, even if mobility is your strong point.

Stained-water situations also mean great opportunity for jigging spoons. More color, sound, vibration, and action are required to help walleye simply locate food under circumstances of diminished visual acuity. The perimeter of affected water, the range in which a lure or bait can influence the behavior of a fish, is greatly constricted in lakes with cloudy, stained, or dirty water. In environments where walleye experience reduced visual perception, auditory (sound) and olfactory (scent) receptors remain uncompromised, making a strong case for involving jigging spoons tipped with live or scented artificial bait.

The greatest mistake in using jigging spoons for walleye is choosing one that's too big. Many companies make spoons of the same model in several sizes to attract not only walleye, but also other species such as lake trout and northern pike. Packaging for these products is often universal, touting the lure's application for walleye, bass, northern, crappie, muskie, lake trout, catfish, bullhead, sheepshead, and sturgeon, or at least something to that effect, but the size of the spoon dictates which species will actually try to eat it. Larger spoons might get you an aggressive walleye, but relying upon the basic tenet of ice fishing—smaller is better—will improve results in most situations. As a general rule, go slightly larger when fishing water with decreased clarity, but overall keep the spoons relatively small.

Jigging spoons offer a powerful attractive property: visual appeal. Yet a highly influential characteristic for ice fishing is scent and flavor. This means more than the spoon is required to catch larger quantities of fish, regardless of the species you're targeting.

Live-bait options include minnow heads, whole minnows, and larvae. Summer options like leeches and nightcrawlers are no longer available, and creative anglers who pamper such creatures to survive for winter use find their effectiveness null. Minnows and larvae simply produce much better.

If choosing to hang a minnow head on the hook of a spoon, one of the most productive options for catching winter walleye, pinch the head off instead of using a knife. Although your hands will get messy, the

■ Eater-size walleye are on the menu for many ice anglers. A small spoon and minnow head tempted this fish, but the opportunity to catch dinner may have passed if the presentation was much larger.

scent released into the water is much more substantial via fingers than with tools.

Anglers wanting to keep their hands clean often opt for artificial attractors pinned to the end of a spoon. Soft plastic-tails like Lindy's Munchies Tiny Tails or Berkley's Powerbait Micros are effective and easy to store—no worries about freezing.

Three spoons cover the gamut of applications, even when looking at various species. Lindy's Flyer, Frostee, and Rattl'r spoons each have a unique action of their own to tempt big walleye, and these spoons really whomp on the walleye!

Yet there will be times when walleye are a little "off." Maybe the conditions aren't right or the ice is creating excessive rumbling due to expansion. Certain circumstances call for more than just a great spoon—technique determines success! These reaction-inducing methods are your gateway to icing winter walleye, even when the fish are less than active.

Split-Shot Walleye

Another standard ice fishing option for walleye is a simple hook-and-sinker combination, often called the "split-shot rig."

JIGGING SPOON TECHNIQUES FOR WALLEYE

Hit-and-Sit. Summer anglers commonly contact the bottom. Some jigging techniques actually work best with a constant connection to the substrate. Yet for some reason ice anglers commonly suspend their baits in the clear blue of the water column.

Using a spoon, rapidly jig with a 2- to 4-inch range of motion. Periodically drop the spoon to the bottom and let it lay stationary for several seconds. Wary walleye will approach and stare at the motionless bait. Once the angler finally lifts the spoon, the observing fish reacts, striking instinctively without hesitation.

The Shake. Shaking a spoon involves super-concentrated movements of the rod-tip—often in an area of less than an inch. The goal is to keep the body of the spoon essentially still while making the hook flip and flit. Using a small worm or white soft plastic trailer like the Lindy Tiny Tails or Powerbait Micros impersonates the white flashes of a fledgling minnow's belly.

Rip-and-Slip. Long, fast upward motions rip the spoon through the water, creating flash, vibration, and bubbles that attract walleye from great distances. However, inactive fish often follow their final approach with abrupt departure. That's when it's time to slip a different, smaller bait in front of the fish. The spoon acts as the attractor while the smaller bait finalizes a response from wary walleye.

Begin by attaching a size 4 live-bait hook to the end of your line. Then pinch a small split-shot sinker to the line a few inches above the hook. Placement of this sinker in relation to hook proximity dictates how far your minnow will be able to "roam." The sinker acts as an anchor or pivot point, and if the sinker is sitting 6 inches above your hook, your minnow will be able to swim 6 inches away from your sinker in a 360-degree circumference. Moving the sinker closer to the hook shortens the span, so the minnow is in a much more confined area. Varying the sinker placement to discover a preferred appearance works, but can be difficult when the fish are negative in attitude. For years, anglers have voiced the theory that active walleye prefer a greater length between the hook and sinker, while neutral or negative fish gravitate toward a shorter tether. This isn't always the case, but generally provides some reasonable parameters.

If using a smaller minnow, such as a fathead or crappie minnow, then a like-size number 6 hook is more applicable. Conversely, very large minnows such as huge golden shiners or sucker minnows require a larger hook, and a size 2 may work much better. The right size and type of minnow can often mean the difference between catching fish or not. If ever in doubt of what to choose, start small and work your way up. Smaller minnows are suitable forage for the greatest size range of walleye.

Selecting an appropriate line weight is extremely important with the split-shot rig, since the natural movements generated by the minnow are what attract the fish. Walleye visually detect heavy line quite easily, and the greater weight and diameter of heavy line can force the minnow to work harder while swimming. Imagine trying to jump rope using clothesline string versus a logging rope. The latter would undoubtedly cause an average human to tire quite rapidly! Unless you've been secretly training Olympian-caliber bait, your minnow is no different. Plainly stated, light line allows greater movement and range of motion when using live bait.

Bait-and-Switch Walleye—Enticing Scattered Fish from Afar

Fifteen minutes of daylight. Six items on the list of things to do at home. Two lines in the water. *One* fish on your mind, and you have yet to get a bite.

Frustrating? Sometimes. When the bite is on, there is a feeling of excitement yet tranquility, but when fishing's slow, aggravation sets in. Schools of wandering walleye mean more fish in the hole at a time and an increased level of competition among the fish. This rivalry equates to action for the angler. But not today. A thick blanket of snow, extremely cold temperatures, and scattered fish make anglers second-guess their reasoning for venturing out. However, that's about to change.

Successful walleye anglers understand the fish-catching potential of both artificial and live-bait presentations. Live bait typically outperforms hard-water lures when walleye are sluggish—yet don't underestimate the impact of using both simultaneously, incorporating the best of both worlds, especially when fish are spread out and seemingly unresponsive.

The bait-and-switch—terminology used to describe the business act of luring customers into the store by offering an exceptional deal on one item, then replacing it with a different product at a higher price—is exactly what astute anglers do to convince lethargic walleye to bite.

The "bait" in this scenario is a flashy, active artificial lure to bring fish into close proximity. Since much of ice fishing entails attracting fish to the immediate vicinity, even with angler mobility taken into consideration, walleye or any other species need some visual temptation. When water clarity and ambient light diminish, fish have more difficulty with visual acuity. A small, gently hooked minnow swimming furiously may be exactly what walleye want to eat, but they first have to find it. Enter the "bait."

■ Walleye approach from great distances when the right bait is on the table. Lures that imitate minnows, like this pair of Salmo Chubby Darters, provide the look of natural forage, but vibrate wickedly to call in fish from afar.

Using an artificial lure, like Salmo's Chubby Darter, calls fish in from a distance. The vibration exhibited during both the ascent and descent when ripped invokes curiosity from far-off walleye. Once this happens, you're already at an advantage; the fish is swimming faster and its sensory receptors are at a heightened state. However, due to the overall level of lassitude, this fish sits, just beneath your jigging efforts, watching, but not really *wanting*. Time for the switch.

If you are comfortable using two rods simultaneously, your second line should already be in the water suspended beneath a hole just a few feet away. In fact, closer is better. Otherwise, quickly reel up the Chubby Darter and drop your minnow.

Using the Lindy Bobber Bug, a pre-tied slip bobber rig with a small jig, bead, and flashy blade, drop the minnow just above the waiting walleye. If your Bobber Bug is already in the next hole over, simply crank up the Chubby Darter and give your minnow a subtle twitch to make sure it's swimming. You've gotten the fish to approach; now fool it with the scent and live action of the minnow.

It's easiest to perform the bait-and-switch with two rods simultaneously in the water. Drill three holes in a line, just a few inches to a foot apart, and drop the Bobber Bug and Chubby Darter down the outside holes. Now place the Ice-Ducer from your Vexilar flasher in the center hole. You will be able to observe both baits on the display while your Ice-Ducer remains segregated in the center hole, eliminating the need to pull the Ice-Ducer float out while battling a big fish.

The Lindy Bobber Bug won't need much for action, so your live-bait rod can sit in a holder while the minnow attractively swims. However, a slip float attached to the live-bait presentation provides more flexibility for the angler. Even though you can see the Bobber Bug and minnow on the Vexilar display, a Thill balsa float allows the angler to leave extra line between the rod tip and float. This subsequently provides a tension-free opportunity for the fish to swim with the bait, while allowing extra time for the angler to gain some composure before setting the hook once a cautious walleye falls for the old bait-and-switch.

CHAPTER SIX

Northern Pike through the Ice

Situated at the top of the food chain in most freshwater ecosystems, northern pike are one of the main predators to other fish. With rows of razor-sharp teeth, northern pike leave telltale signs of their aggressive nature on the sides of

■ The sleek body, tooth-filled jaw, and camouflaged coloring of a northern pike make it one of freshwater's fiercest predators. While some species become increasingly lethargic beneath the ice, pike activity heightens.

prey lucky enough to escape following an attack. Anglers losing pike on minnows can often identify the species without ever seeing the fish due to the slashes and gashes marking the bait.

Northern pike seem to have some of the most interesting nicknames of all freshwater species: hammer-handles, slime-darts, gators, jacks, stinkies, and simply "pike" all refer to the lesser sizes of the terrific trophy fish.

While some other species become lethargic in cold water, northern pike don't seem to lose their affinity for stalking prey and striking with fury. Brightly colored, flashy presentations partnered with assertive movement attract northern pike.

The pike's anatomical configuration is ideal for ambushing prey: a long, slender body with wide fins, aerodynamic from end to end, and rows of razor sharp teeth powered by vise-like jaws used to hold a fish, then systematically turn the prey to swallow it whole. Northerns don't chew their food thirty times like a human, but instead use the rows of teeth to guide the prey into their throat.

Popular Pike Gear

Choosing appropriate northern pike gear is a compromise between personal preference, affordability, and functionality. Since northern pike can become quite substantial in size, rods, reels, and line should be comparably hefty. Anglers have a choice between spinning and baitcasting outfits (although no casting is required while ice fishing). Tip-ups are another viable option and create a multi-line setup. Typically, anglers choose either spinning reels or tip-ups for hard-water northerns. Even though baitcasting reels have great features for fishing northerns, super-cold temperatures wreak havoc on the line guide and pawl, the mechanism that pans back and forth to evenly distribute the line onto your spool. However, tepid air temperature or the warmth of a heated shanty provides the necessary environment for using a baitcasting outfit.

Fishing line for spinning and baitcasting reels, as well as tip-ups, should be strong and resistant to abrasion. Since pike have super-sharp teeth that can shred prey and components instantly, steel leaders are often used. Yet sophisticated ice anglers know that even though steel protection may help to land a pike once it strikes, the occurrence of aggressive hits may decrease due to the noticeable wire's easy detection. Other options exist to thwart cut lines, including braided lines and fluorocarbon leaders. Because braided line and those classified as "super" lines are composed of numerous separate strands of filament jointly entwined to form a durable, abrasion-resistant unit, anglers can tie directly to a lure. Are braided line and superline the ultimate answer to getting cut off? No, but there is a decrease in the number of times your poor, frost-fearing fingers will need to leave the comfort of insulated gloves to re-tie a severed line. Superlines definitely

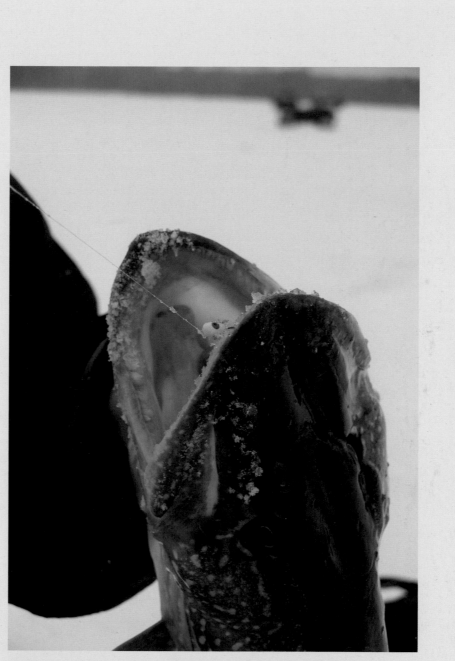

■ Northern pike terrorize smaller fish and often lurk within vegetation to pounce upon prey. A panfish angler was lucky enough to land this one with a crappie jig, but the razor-sharp teeth typically slice through light line.

hold up better against a northern pike's continuous rows of razor-sharp teeth.

Tip-ups

Several tip-up designs are available to aid in the quest for northern pike. Each angler has a personal preference, choosing between conventional wood frame tip-ups, circular designs, pop-ups, X-frames, and the standard rectangular resin frame. Another option includes "rod holder" tip-ups that incorporate an ice fishing rod and

reel into a frame, allowing the angler to fight the fish instead of hauling it in hand over hand.

Windlass tip-ups fall within the category of tip-ups, although they function slightly differently. A standard tip-up relies entirely upon the action of the minnow to attract fish. Checking the minnow periodically for liveliness is mandatory. Yet the windlass tip-up harnesses the breeze, gently moving the hook up and down, providing motion even after the minnow

■ Tip up! Watching a flag trip as the spindle churns at high speed puts the angler in hot pursuit. Tip-ups prove valuable for many species, but remain most popular for anglers chasing *Esox lucius*, commonly known as northern pike.

has lost its enthusiasm. Anglers that use frozen smelt prefer the unattended movement provided by the windlass tip-up for attracting pike.

Setting your minnow at the appropriate depth, once a combination of research and guesswork, is now a simple task while incorporating your electronics. Every angler has his or her own formula for attaining accurate depth adjustment. Some attach a clip-on weight to the hook and drop the mass to the bottom, calculating the distance by arm's length and subtracting a few feet for a near-bottom position. Others simply drop their line and rely upon faith.

Today anglers simply use their flasher to watch the bait as it descends through the frigid water. This enables accurate positioning just above weed tops where northern pike are able to see your presentation from a greater distance. It is common to see a northern approach on the display as the minnow initially falls. Clip-on weights,

■ **Circle, Kahle, and 90-degree minnow hooks all sufficiently harness a minnow tethered to a tip-up. Pairing larger hooks with larger minnows and smaller hooks with smaller minnows permits the bait to swim naturally yet solidly hold the fish upon hook-set.**

also known as "depth finders," relay an acceptable approximation of depth, but don't indicate the presence of weeds. Any angler who has ever deployed a minnow beneath a tip-up and walked away, only to discover a deep-sixed minnow after an hour or two has passed, can relate to the frustration. Pike will occasionally pick up a struggling fish or dead minnow lying atop matted weeds, but they usually do not rummage beneath the weeds to find food.

Hooks for Tip-Ups. Choosing the appropriate size hook for your minnow is easier than choosing a particular style of hook in the tackle aisle. Many anglers choose a standard live-bait hook or kahle-style hook for use with tip-ups. These are two good choices. Two other options are circle hooks and square-bend hooks. Originally created for saltwater application, circle hooks have crossed over to freshwater ice fishing. When a fish takes a circle hook and minnow attached to a tip-up, the angler doesn't set the hook but instead simply tightens the line. A circle hook typically secures the fish in the corner of its mouth, causing less internal harm while providing a greater likelihood of a successful release.

Square-bend hooks simply have two 90-degree bends instead of a conventional, gradual curve. These work best for larger, wide minnows.

Swedish pike hooks, once thought to be the best option for using big minnows, tend to cause substantial harm to the fish and result in a high mortality rate. Even small, pestering pike deserve a chance to grow larger if catch-and-release is your intent. Keeping a few pike to eat is just fine, but having a fish die due to angler error upon release is unfortunate.

Handheld Equipment

Medium-format spinning and baitcasting reels for pike have strong components needed to not only battle the large predator, but also do so effectively in sub-zero environments. Slightly longer ice fishing rods provide better leverage, resulting in more successful hook sets. An overly stout rod redirects the pressure from the impact absorbent blank of the rod to the line, resulting in additional stress that sometimes results in lost fish or a broken line.

Pairing the appropriate rod and reel together is important no matter what species you're after, but in addition to the seemingly scientific categories of balance and action, there is a major detail to aid in performance: Spinning and baitcasting reels function best when paired with rods of similar design. It sounds logically basic, but the common practice of mismatching components is frequent. Maybe someday a rod manufacturer will design a bilateral model that functions properly with either a spinning or baitcasting reel. For now, that is not an option, and in reality, it's not in the angler's best interest. Reel seat orientation, blank design, and components determine the specific use of a rod. The oversize line guides with elongated arms on a spinning rod accommodate the wide rotation of a spinning reel's retrieve. When inverted, the line no longer follows the contour of the rod in a smooth, linear fashion, but instead bends at sharp angles, placing more pressure on the line as it passes through the guides. In other words, attaching a baitcasting reel to a spinning rod does not work. On the other hand, using a spinning reel on a baitcasting rod likewise causes complications. First, the line guides are not large enough to provide the space needed for letting out line and retrieval, resulting in a rod that wobbles violently when cranking line onto the spool. Second, the trigger that provides a nice handle for a solid grip on a baitcasting rod sticks straight up when paired with a spinning reel. Maybe you don't mind having the trigger protrude into the palm of your hand all afternoon, but this additionally affects the sensitivity you gain from having your hand on the rod handle.

Finding Big Pike

Unlike massive schools of bluegill, crappie, or even wandering walleye, pike are solitary creatures. Their worries are minimal, with the exception of anglers. Situated at the top of the food chain, northern pike terrorize the lives of any smaller fish swimming in the same lake and assist in fisheries management by preventing panfish populations from overcrowding. Smaller fish live in constant alert, wondering what might be lurking behind or positioned around the next turn.

Though northern pike don't school, certain areas garnish numbers of pike. Flourishing weed beds, flats, rocky points, and drop-offs put pike in the position for attack. Yet trophy-caliber pike set themselves apart from areas inundated with smaller fish of the same species. Big northerns wait in the wings, just beyond the skirts of activity, waiting for the perfect moment to engage.

Lakes that support northern pike range from shallow, grassy prairie potholes to massively expansive deepwater giants. The majority of lakes dotting the Midwest contain pike, but not every body of water contains big northerns. A strong forage supply provides the needed sustenance to develop large fish. Small lakes usually have the proper elements to support a few big pike, whereas larger bodies of water typically hold greater numbers.

Structure is of great importance to pike, and lakes with diverse terrain better accommodate their needs. Early in the spring, when lakes begin to lose their ice cap, northern pike wander into marshy backwaters to spawn. Traveling toward small tributaries and scantly navigable ditches, reproduction takes place in water less than a few feet deep. Lakes lacking these spawning arenas do not have great numbers of northern pike due to limited natural reproduction; yet don't discount their potential for large fish. Even though the flag on your tip-up won't spring every few minutes, there is still an opportunity for big fish due to limited competition.

■ Locations with high numbers of panfish often have northern pike lurking in the vicinity. However, panfish-size equipment isn't your best choice for battling trophies like this. BILL LINDNER

Northern pike prefer various types of cover, but favor fancy vegetation more than any other option. Weeds allow the fish to hide from their prey, darting out at the last second, viciously attacking unsuspecting prey. The location of pike can change throughout the course of the winter, but some basic areas commonly hold fish. Sprawling shallow weed flats and weed-line drop-offs create the most desirable habitat for pike.

Setting up camp on hallowed pike grounds is every angler's goal. Strategically placing your tip-ups in a couple holes and waiting for the flags to pop (in the same way an archery hunter watches from a deer stand) is relaxing, but isn't the best way to maximize your success. No one would argue that grilling bratwurst on the ice while simultaneously catching a handful of pike doesn't sound like an enjoyable afternoon. Yet hyper-focused pike protagonists know the secret to catching more and bigger northerns: mobility. Tip-ups allow an angler to use multiple lines where legal, but fishing a mediocre area for hours on end results in mediocre success.

Stalking pike instead of waiting for their arrival proves advantageous for the angler. Pounding out twenty or more holes in a small area is common practice for bluegill fishing, and an all-out approach for northern pike isn't any different. Thirty holes might be more accurate. Okay, let's make it forty. In other words, explore. Move. Experiment.

When Size Matters

Minnesota, situated as one of the most popular ice fishing destinations, was once a northern pike mecca. Trophy fish were the focus, and postcard photos reflected their popularity. Beer commercials portrayed anglers battling a massive pike, then grilling it over an open flame. Ah, to live the High Life.

Today northern pike fishing throughout much of the state is different, but change lingers on the horizon. A movement is taking place, implemented by the Minnesota Department of Natural Resources in conjunction with lake associations and fueled by a common interest, to bring northern pike fishing back to its prime.

Doug Kingsley, Department of Natural Resources (DNR) Area Fisheries supervisor in the quaint northern Minnesota town of Park Rapids, says that increasing the size of northern pike on regional lakes takes conscious effort. Experimental regulations and conscientious angling practices both positively influence northern pike abundance.

"Northern pike reproduction in certain bodies of water is fairly limited," says Kingsley. Yet this smaller overall population actually provides a unique opportunity to foster larger-than-average northern pike because of less competition for natural food sources, which results in better overall growth.

A few impacting factors decrease a lake's potential for producing larger-than-typical northern pike. One is angler harvest

■ Tullibee provide forage for big fish in larger lakes, and ample populations produce larger-than-average northern pike. This one escaped with its life, but not before feeling the toothy bite of a hungry predator.

of big fish. "People commonly want to keep larger northerns versus smaller ones," says Kingsley, who suggests keeping northern pike "as small as you're willing to fillet." A lake with too much natural reproduction will show signs of stunting over time, since the natural forage base does not provide enough food for many fish to grow large.

The life cycle of a northern pike begins when spawning takes place in spring. As the ice melts, adult pike wander into seasonally flooded wetlands to lay their eggs on vegetative mats. After an incubation period of twelve to fourteen days, the offspring hatch, initially subsisting on nutrients provided from the egg sac. The immature pike progress to zooplankton and, after a short period, feed upon minnow fry of various natures. Northern pike three to six years old are generally the most abundant and productive spawners, commonly measuring 18 to 30 inches in length. As the fish age beyond that point, their fertility begins to diminish.

So what can anglers do to increase their odds of catching a pike worthy of trophy status in the future? First, become familiar with the experimental regulations for specific bodies of water. These management slots reduce harvest of larger-than-average fish, allowing the overall size to increase, which takes considerable time. Kingsley says the DNR evaluates impact from experimental regulations frequently, but results only become noticeable after ten to twelve years. The duration varies by species, but for northern pike, change occurs slowly. Kingsley notes that an eight-year-old northern pike within his management sector is "getting pretty old."

The second act anglers can perform to increase numbers of big fish is practicing selective harvest. This entails keeping smaller northern pike while releasing medium to large fish. By doing so, the population of larger fish will increase and the encounters with "hammer handles" will drop. And who knows, maybe you'll be asked to star in a beer commercial if you're lucky.

CHAPTER SEVEN

Ice Fishing for Crappie

Whereas bluegills require a rather finite tackle selection, an arsenal for crappie mirrors the expansive size of this fish's mouth. Tiny, super-finesse jigs such as teardrops and ants comprise the smaller end of tackle required for crappie, while mid-size spoons and artificial lures readily fit into the gaping maw of

■ Crappies are a popular target for ice anglers. Found both shallow and deep, big crappie favor flashy minnow imitators and tiny jigs tipped with maggots.

a hungry slab, further diversifying your tackle box.

Crappies are particularly fond of small minnows, and likewise imitators are a necessity for any serious crappie angler. Yet don't discount the effectiveness of tiny jigs that emulate native invertebrates.

Though color undoubtedly plays a role in the crappie's fondness for your bait, each lake, and sometimes individual fish, differ in color preference. Trial-and-error remains beneficial when searching for the "hot color."

It seems that nearly every tackle manufacturer offers a line of baits with radiant-glow potential in a variety of color options ranging from the original off-white hue to extremes of blue, green, and red. There is no need to find your inner artist, since locating glow-in-the-dark paint is actually more difficult than purchasing a pre-painted glow jig.

Utilizing luminescent baits after dark is presumably the ideal time to capitalize upon their ability to contrast and be seen against a dark background. Nevertheless, people tend to overlook the subtle feature of a glow bait used in the middle of the day. The extreme contrast after dark can sometimes be, well, "glow-verload." Think of all the subtleties anglers pay attention to while using other baits throughout the year—changing factory rings and hooks on crankbaits for the perfect size, trimming skirts on jigs and spinnerbaits, bending hooks for just the right angle—but never contemplating controlling the light and color emitted by a glow-bait for ice fishing. Since most baits recharge their glow-ability in about twenty seconds, anglers typically go for the maximum allotted time to make the bait stand out. Yet keep in mind that pitch-black situations require less light to create a drastic appearance.

Think of turning on a flashlight outdoors in the middle of a clear sunny day, on a cloudy day, and in the middle of the night. Three different formats affect visual perception of identical light intensity due to the ambient light available in the immediate environment.

Now approach the same concept from the perspective of a fish beneath the ice. For most of the winter, their underwater world is dark, or at least much darker than compared to the open-water season. Snow sitting atop the ice doesn't allow much light to penetrate into the water, and as the snow gets deeper, even less light passes. A bright sunny day provides opportunity to utilize the effectiveness of a glow bait, even in clear water. The soft glow of a jig may be the answer to trigger a bite from a finicky spectator.

Water clarity becomes another important factor when considering the use of glow baits. Humans can see quite a distance on land, but even the keen-eyed walleye has decreased visual acuity in stained water. Offering luminescent bait charged below a Lindy Tazer for a few seconds provides all species of fish a simple avenue for locating your presentation visually. Even in the middle of the day!

■ The attractive appearance of a glow-in-the-dark bait gains attention from all species of fish. Although anglers commonly charge their glow baits during low-light periods, decreased ambient light below the ice creates a niche for utilizing luminescent baits all day long.

Leaving Live Bait for Synthetic Simulation

The popularity of artificial bait is on the rise. Most bass anglers rely exclusively upon those fashioned from wood, rubber, and composite materials, while many devout muskie aficionados consider live bait to be an unfair advantage. Professional walleye anglers continue to explore the capabilities of artificial bait, holding tournaments where artificial lures are encouraged while continuing to amass huge daily limits of fish.

However, one arena has been slow to warm up to the idea of presenting a hook void of live bait: ice fishing. Of course, that is, until now.

It's no secret that fish underneath winter's ice canopy are sleepwalking compared to the aggressive nature displayed during late June and early July. Lethargic, yes. Inactive, no! Anyone who has needed a hemostat to dislodge a ¼-ounce jigging spoon from the gullet of a full-bellied crappie can attest to that. These fish are ready to feed, especially if an easy opportunity presents itself. However, a winter fish craves a plastic differing from a sure-fire summer presentation. A ¹⁄₁₆-ounce jig head with a plastic tail works great for big panfish and the occasional gamefish during summer months, but winter tactics call for the ultimate in finesse. This applies to plastic as well.

Scent, texture, flavor, and movement vary between live bait and plastic. Just because the two are different does not necessarily mean that one is better than the other. Understanding the potential strength of each arrangement is the first step in creating an artificial presentation that outperforms live bait. For instance, Berkley Power Wigglers look like

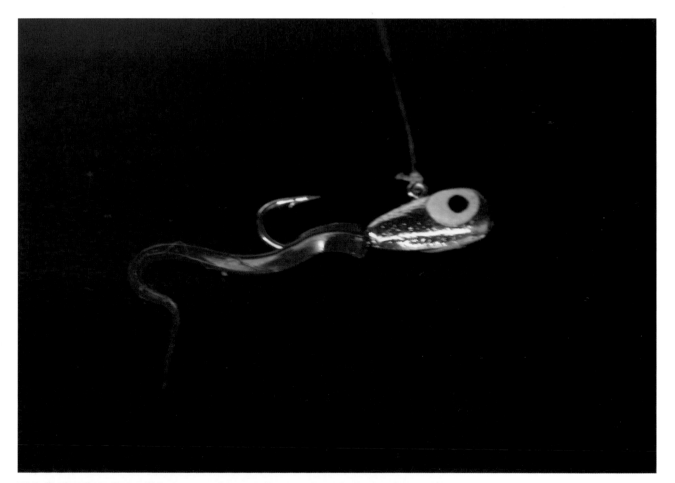

■ Soft plastic trailers, like the one shown delicately threaded onto this ice jig, remain flexible in cold water. The undulating action of such artificial attractors not only catches fish, but virtually eliminates the need to rebait, allowing anglers to keep their hands inside warm gloves.

waxworms or larvae but, if singly hooked through the end, don't have the flexibility of a waxworm when jigged. However, the Power Wiggler maintains its original circumference when threaded on the hook, while a waxworm might burst and become flat. The artificial Power Wiggler will last through more bites, allowing you to keep your bait in the water longer, as well as your hands in your warm gloves.

Lindy Tackle Company has also stepped forward to create a series of superb plastic baits that are perfect for finesse ice fishing. This too is a welcome advantage for ice anglers wanting to avoid cold fingers and sawdust-filled pockets. The baits, called Munchies Tiny Tails, come in four designs and various colors, but simply purchasing the bait won't put fish in the bucket. A few suggestions will increase the productivity of this live-bait alternative.

Lindy Munchies Tiny Tails are advantageous because they are not heavily scented, but once you see them undulate in the water, you'll understand why their effectiveness is superior. To reach maximum visual appeal, be sure to thread the soft plastic tail straight on the hook. If it's crooked, the bait will gradually spin in circles while jigged, causing the fish to question the bait instead of approaching to attack.

Second, the Munchies Tiny Tails function best when subtly jigged. Minimal movement of the rod tip will primarily make the tail pulsate, while more pronounced jerking causes the entire bait to hop and dance. Both techniques will produce in specific situations, but the only way to determine which jigging motion the fish desire is trial-and-error. But once that magic combination is discovered, you'll thank your little plastic-tailed friend every time you catch another fish!

Traditional Crappie Pursuits

Crappies, by nature, are deepwater-loving creatures. Numerous forage opportunities exist in deep water, permitting crappie to feed at will. Crappie will suspend to feed upon zooplankton and roaming schools of minnows, but additionally sit near the bottom, looking for worms and insects present there.

Hard bottoms aren't nearly as attractive to crappie as soft, silt-covered substrates. Most commonly found in deeper, basin-type areas, nearly every lake has a population of deep-roaming crappie, no matter the season.

Hard-bottom areas are relatively easy to find using the flasher to show a double echo, indicating hard structure below, most often over the crest of a hump or point. Following the drop-off, silt-laden regions begin at the base of the primary or secondary break. This is where deepwater crappies reside and is a high-percentage area for anglers.

Unfortunately, specific depths do not consistently produce crappie on every lake. Every body of water differs regarding the location of fish, the depth of the water, and overall size. Some lakes simply don't contain high numbers or respectable sizes of crappie. Predation by larger fish or anglers curbs crappie numbers. However, don't entirely discount a lake due to its average size or numeration. Since lakes experience natural ebb and flow in terms of fish numbers and size, a few strong year classes can positively enhance crappie fishing. This is true of every fish species.

Finding deep, soft bottom doesn't always ensure a productive bite or big fish.

Even though crappie travel in schools, smaller fish may comprise the "base" of a school, with some larger fish mixed in. Landing a few of the larger slabs requires slight changes, typically moving the bait slightly above or below a school of fish.

Since crappies relating to soft bottom are generally deep fish, compact yet heavy jigs allow a fast drop to the proper depth and additionally stretch the fishing line to provide better sensitivity for light biters.

■ Crappie experience a natural cycle that affects size and overall population on many lakes, especially smaller bodies of water. Catch-and-release helps reestablish strong populations on lakes with poor numbers and smaller fish.

Pursuing Shallow-Water Populations

Ice fishing for crappie has become a wild escapade throughout the Midwest. Numerous bodies of water have become meccas, and with the discovery of prolific populations like those inhabiting northern Minnesota's Red Lake, anglers have become converts dedicated to seeking out black-and-white schools of slabs. Fish house cities pop up faster than microwave Orville Redenbacher, each shanty jockeying for position over deepwater schools of fish.

Getting lost in the crowd is fine when fish are biting, but when the bite is slow, do you stick with your plan through the typical prime period of activity, hoping the fish "turn on," or do you pull up stakes and refocus your efforts? The choice is a gamble if you intend to bring home dinner. You could (a) stay put, (b) seek out another lake, concentrating on identical areas that have proven successful in the past, or (c) traverse the current expanse of frozen water to find untouched populations in a varying environment.

Good anglers explore the current populated waters, yet tend to focus upon areas with limited fishing pressure. While groups of people hit flats and open-water expanses, probing the water column with dangling minnows fighting the resistance of a hook in 15 to 35 feet of water, numerous active fish will inhabit water less than 12 feet deep. At times crappies will move up into extremely shallow water, with only 3 feet of breathing room between tall stalks of vegetation and the bottom of the ice. The key, however, is the presence of a food source.

What other component makes a good shallow-water location? Weeds! You'll want the greenest vegetation available, and tall weeds are best. The challenge is finding weed growth that is prolific in the proper location. The weeds should be adjacent to an underwater point or sprawling across a flat. When exploring large weed flats, look for subtleties that stand out on the electronics, as these will often appeal to a fish. Inside turns, increased or decreased vegetative proliferation, and change in bottom content may seem insignificant, but slight to moderate variations characterize productive areas.

When examining points, key areas include small, isolated weed clumps that are shallow but close in proximity to deep water. The fish will dump off to deep water if there is danger, or to simply search for food, which is the typical scenario. If the shallow-water zone already includes provisions, the crappies don't have much of an excuse to leave. When the crappies take residence in shallow areas, they typically sit right in the weeds, as opposed to suspending above vegetation. By using an Aqua-Vu underwater camera, you can see fish mixed in with the weed stalks, hoping an unsuspecting minnow will wander past. Yet many times a minnow on a hook won't get as much attention as the incorporation of a jigging spoon. The Lindy Rattl'r spoon is an excellent choice since the combination

■ Small to medium-size jigging spoons work wonders for enticing shallow-water crappie. Shaking the presentation just above the peak of protruding vegetation garners attention from big slabs.

of noise and vibration alerts an aggressive crappie from a distance, despite the visual hindrance created by obstructive weeds.

Hook a larva one time beneath the head so it dangles beneath the hook, and shake the Rattl'r spoon above the weeds. You'll be high in the water column, sometimes only an arm's length below the ice. Attempt to keep the body of the spoon stable, making the worm and hook dance as you shake your rod. Don't stop! Keep

going until you feel nothing, as the fish will rapidly rise and lift your spoon when they attack. The only thing you'll "feel" is the absence of tension.

A Vexilar FL-20 flasher is ideal for determining proper depth alignment and the presence of fish buried within the vegetation. When using a Vexilar for this technique, you'll visually observe a crappie's expedient vertical rate of travel, hitting the spoon hard and subsequently

■ Shallow water affects the visible area for both angler and fish. Using a flasher in shallow situations remains greatly advantageous, but fish aren't seen on the display until they're tight to your bait. Conversely, fish visual fields equally reduce, since there is less vertical space for viewing.

bringing the bait a few inches toward the surface. Again, this lack of weight indicates the presence of a fish.

Many times, you'll have bluegills approach the spoon, but examine the activity on your electronics, and you'll notice them hanging under your bait until you pause from jigging. Highly aggressive and large bluegills will attack the Rattl'r spoon without hesitation, so be prepared to fight some bruisers looking for more than a mouthful! Since weedy areas are often a bluegill's first choice for location, expect to land more greedy sunfish than you would in deeper locations.

Other times, the spoon will attract fish, either bluegills or crappies, into close proximity, but their already-full bellies may play a role in their decision to bite. Turn uncertainty into an opportunity by keeping another rod close by rigged with a smaller bait and lighter line, as the lesser offering may turn out to be a huge crappie's after dinner mint and your answer to landing shallow-water slabs.

Deepwater Expeditions

Locating deepwater crappie requires more than simply finding 20 to 40 feet of water. Crappies inhabit areas for a variety of reasons, but rarely for depth alone. Food and accommodating conditions are more important to slabs. So how does an angler determine which areas have the greatest potential, especially on the maiden voyage to a new lake? First off, consider seasonal movements of the fish. Crappie often position themselves in shallow water during early ice periods since there's ample oxygen and readily available forage. This isn't always the case, but another key in identifying crappie location begins weeks before the ice actually forms. Finding crappie via boat late in the fall is an asset, since those fish commonly remain nearby into the early ice season.

A little information goes a long way in the pursuit for deepwater fish. Fishing reports can point you in the right direction, but don't expect to limit-out over the lunch hour. Deepwater crappie typically become active as the sun falls from the sky and periodically throughout the night. Early-morning hours are also valuable on particular lakes. But deepwater midday fish are generally hard to come by.

Begin your quest for deepwater crappie with a lake map and look toward points, humps, and expansive flats near basins. Main-lake basins often possess the necessary attributes for schools of crappie, but some lakes provide better opportunities for fish and anglers alike in smaller arms and bays with deep holes.

Bottom type plays an important role in the search for deepwater crappie. Softer substrates house the tiny creatures that crappie love. Clouds of zooplankton are another favorite, and minnows additionally feed on the miniature organisms. Crappies have an affinity for minnows, and the multiple food sources keep schools of fish in an area for long periods.

■ On certain lakes, monster crappie school in deep water, giving anglers good reason to explore drop-offs, basins, and main-lake flats.

■ Deepwater crappie love both minnows and maggots. A compact yet heavy jig like the Lindy Fat Boy, shown here, provides a fast descent to the waiting fish and better contact with the bait while jigging and detecting light bites.

Anglers targeting deepwater crappie have multiple presentation options. A crappie minnow dangling from a bare hook or small jig is a simple presentation that doesn't require much along the lines of technique—the minnow does all the work. One word of caution: The weight of a jig or split-shot requires the minnow to work harder to move, diminishing the swimming area and resulting in rapid exhaustion. Many anglers prefer a tiny, bare hook with a split-shot or two pinched onto the line 3 or 4 inches above the hook, allowing the minnow to swim around the perimeter of the weight.

Small panfish jigs tipped with one or more maggots is another favorite for crappie both shallow and deep. However, in deeper water, heavy yet compact jigs work best. The additional weight allows the bait to drop to the fish quickly and tightens the fishing line, providing better contact with the bait while feeling for a light bite or giving the bait some action. Yet careful selection of a compact, heavy jig for crappie involves finding one with a small hook and larger head. As jig sizes increase, hook size often follows accordingly, but certain jigs, like Lindy's Fat Boy, have a heavier head and small hook, the perfect presentation for deep crappie.

Sonar electronics are a huge asset when fishing deep water for crappie. Since pairs, trios, and compact schools of slabs wander through the water column at various depths, the angler must remain flexible in vertical position. In certain situations, crappie may relate to the bottom, hovering just a few feet above the mud or silt. Yet fish passing several feet above your bait won't typically descend to take the offering. Pinpointing these fish in the upper portion of the water column is simple with a flasher, and raising the presentation to the proper level only requires a keen eye on the flasher and a few cranks of the reel handle.

CHAPTER EIGHT

The Search for Perch

Sought by legions of comparably nomadic anglers, perch are cruisers of the underwater world. Following schools of minnows, ransacking shallow-water haunts, and ultimately scouring the lake for food, perch have a penchant for eating.

Perch often reside in areas similar to those inhabited by walleye and may be deemed "pesky" by anglers seeking the larger aforementioned species. However, this isn't always the case. Perch sporadically mingle with other varieties of fish such as bluegill and crappie, but usually congregate in segregated schools.

Locating yellow perch isn't always a simple matter of drilling a hole, then dropping a line. Not every lake contains a healthy population of the species. Some lakes have high numbers of perch, but their average size is minimal. They function dually as a food source; walleye, northern pike, muskie, bass—even large panfish— often prey upon perch. Obviously, perch must be tiny for a bluegill or crappie to engulf, but when other food sources are scarce, a tiny perch suits them just fine.

Availability of various forage types, like perch, contributes to a well-rounded ecosystem, but unfortunately, a lake's biomass isn't always consistent. Fluctuations in predator species population has an effect on forage proliferation. If the population of certain fish species, like walleye for instance, increases exponentially, the overall amount of food consumed by those predators increases. Stable reproduction with an increased average size of walleye results in a similar amplification of forage consumption. Both scenarios can reduce the population of forage species, such as cisco (tullibee), shiners, dace, and perch.

Conversely, decreased predation due to limited reproduction or maturation of the predator species, in this case walleye, allows the forage to flourish. These variations most commonly impact smaller bodies of water, where entire populations per species are less significant and more susceptible.

Perch can become cannibalistic when food is in short supply. This is possible for all species, arising from necessity rather than desire. However, it is a rarity for perch, as they are more apt to rely on small minnows, insect larvae, and miniature worms that exist in and near the bottom.

Large bodies of water with massive flats are definitely lakes to check out for jumbo perch. If there's a substantial walleye population in one of these larger lakes, then there's probably a good perch population to help support it. Yet bigger doesn't necessarily mean better. A number of medium-size lakes, reservoirs, backwaters, and even tiny potholes spattered throughout the various ice fishing regions are enviable perch waters.

Small, shallow ponds usually have relatively murky water with a soft bottom. Lacking the diverse structure present on larger lakes, these secluded waters still produce some huge perch. In other words,

don't write off a lake strictly because of volume.

Medium-size lakes, ranging from about 800 to 2,000 acres, can also have potentially fruitful perch fishing. Yet how do you decide which lake to try? Certain geographic areas have hundreds of lakes within a ten-minute drive. Such diversity presents both opportunity and difficulty. Choosing a lake dependent upon weather conditions is an asset, but with so many choices it's easy to second-guess your destination or feel remorse for deciding to fish a particular lake after an unsuccessful trip. Yet having so many bodies of water within a stone's throw of each other makes

■ Small jigs tipped with one, two, or even several maggots get perch excited when other presentations fail. BILL LINDNER

■ Jigging spoons are popular presentations for stocky perch like this one. Because the presentation is also a walleye favorite and the two species frequent similar areas, be prepared to tangle with the occasional bonus walleye.

Popular Perch Presentations

Successful perch anglers rely upon two types of strategies: active and passive. An active strategy involves plenty of reflection-producing motion. Active strategies aren't necessarily dependent upon presentation size. Producing invigorating action with a small bait is an active approach. Aggressive, insatiable, and competitive mannerisms are characteristic of vivacious perch, and equally animated presentations garner their attention. Jigging spoons are undoubtedly the most popular presentation for active perch, but small jigs tipped with live bait produce when flashy spoons fail—a good backup plan for neutral or negative-attitude perch.

Passive presentations require little, if any, effort by the angler. More commonly relegated to smaller baits, a passive approach follows the idea that less is more. The simplest strategic exhibition of a passive presentation is in direct contact with the bottom. Anglers sometimes catch plump perch after setting their rod on the ice to open a bottle of water.

Ice anglers often keep their bait suspended somewhere between the ice and bottom, dancing their offering around like a marionette. Though small minnows and zooplankton hover in the same region, tiny invertebrates call the bottom home. Perch and other fish species find themselves with their snouts to the lake bed, plucking these small creatures out of the silt, sand, and mud. It's common practice to leave a presentation sitting on the bottom during the open-water season, and ice fishing is no different. Perch, panfish, walleye, and pike all search for food on the bottom, giving reason for ice anglers to occasionally position their presentation in direct contact with the substrate, allowing fish to "root" for their bait.

Locating Ice-Time Perch

A number of structures support and attract perch. Attacking every one of these areas on a decent-size lake within the time constraints of a fishing trip can be impossible. For instance, points, weed edges, shallow flats, deep basins, drop-offs, humps, sandbars, rock piles, and weed clumps are all viable options for catching perch. Sometimes super-subtle changes such as transitions in bottom content become the relevant factor in locating winter perch.

Seeking information by "listening" to the fish and from electronic and human sources (see chapter two, Ice Fishing Gear and Equipment, and chapter three, Ice Electronics) dramatically reduces the time and energy required to catch perch, even though prime fishing potential exists in a multitude of diverse locations.

Listening to the Fish

So many spots, so little time. Running from point to point, flat-to-flat, hump-to-hump, etc., etc., might actually cause you to go insane—not literally, but there simply aren't enough hours in a day to check every area. Instead, begin by using a systematic approach that applies to all species of fish: pair the information you've already gathered about the lake with the general information you possess regarding perch (or other species).

Let's say that anglers have been catching perch all week on the decline of a couple of long points that intersect with a deep basin. You heard the bite was wild on Monday, but prior commitments prevented a fishing trip until Saturday. Now there's plenty of competition from other anglers, and the action is sporadic. It seems like everyone has only a couple decent jumbos tossed in the bucket, and smaller fish are everywhere.

Chasing a hot bite commonly meets this outcome. Pioneering and discovering a bite requires great amounts of time, effort, patience, and a little luck. In this particular situation, the fish may be just as active as they were on Monday, but in another, similar area.

■ Exploring isolated structure not far from popular fishing sites will put perch in your pail while other anglers struggle. Community areas are fine when the bite is "on," but when activity slows, subtleties in the near vicinity and a break from the crowd of anglers often equate to success. RON ANLAUF

The two primary points that everyone is concentrating upon are not going to make this a Saturday to remember. You have two choices: stick it out and hope for a few more perch, or move on. Changing your presentation is a good initial option, but if the action is slow for everyone, there's probably a lack of fish versus ambivalence toward your bait.

Approaching the circumstances as an opportunity rather than a problem mentally prepares the angler to succeed in launching a new plan. Using prior knowledge, a paper map, or GPS, look for isolated areas with similar, less-defined attributes. Smaller points or bars that extend into depths identical to the "popular" points are a good first choice. A comparable terrain decline is another consideration.

Now drill holes in a number of areas relative to the secluded structure. Check along the drop-off in various depths, the base of the primary drop, and on top of the bar. Don't pass on shallow-water areas, assuming perch won't be there.

Super-Shallow Perch

Why would perch inhabit water that's only a couple feet deep? Food! Worms and invertebrates that wiggle and crawl in only a couple feet of water attract schools of hungry perch. Perch greet anglers in shallow water during the first portion of the ice fishing season and again late in the year.

Sprawling shallow flats expanding from the shoreline are common areas to find shallow-water perch. Flashy jigs, spoons, and minnow imitators that produce deepwater perch also perform well for shallow-water perch. Yet vision for both the fish and angler become limited in these areas.

On one hand, it's easier to see bottom in shallow water when staring down an ice hole, but the visible area becomes smaller as water depth gets shallower. These same limitations, although different by anatomical form, also affect visual fields of fish. Since fish see vertically and horizontally in cone-shaped forms, farther distances open a larger visible perimeter that shallow water simply doesn't allow.

Electronics have a smaller visible area in shallow water, too. Flashers "see" downward in an inverted cone that widens with distance. If angling in 4 or 5 feet of water, a fish needs to be very close to your hook before you'll see it on the display.

Pounding for Perch

Perch love activity. Dancing spoons, jiggling jigs, and fledgling minnows attract jumbos to at least watch, if not strike. Their curiosity plays into the angler's hand, and once the fish are within close proximity, the likelihood of capture is high. The flashy finishes and dynamic action of such baits provide easy location for wandering perch in shallow water.

If the general mood of the fish is neutral or negative, they'll need more persuasion than simply jigging, shaking, or dropping a bait. One solution is pounding the bottom with your presentation, and a few specific methods work best.

The first entails dropping the bait to the bottom and letting it sit. When I say "to the bottom," I literally mean allowing your hook to *hit* the bottom, keeping it temporarily motionless. Once the bait hits bottom, it causes a slight disruption of sand, muck, silt, or other bottom type, dependent upon the available substrate. Remain motionless for several seconds so an observant perch can rummage around for your offering. With this technique, the majority of bites occur while the bait is sitting stationary on the bottom.

Another option is repeated pounding. Once again, drop your bait until it contacts the bottom, but now methodically lift and drop the presentation. This particular method can create quite a disruption of the bottom, so be careful not to create a cloud of sediment and debris so dense that it scares fish from the area.

To monitor the level of commotion you're creating, watch carefully using your underwater camera or lie flat on the ice in a sight-fishing position to observe the action.

Don't Be Shy

Their eyes are bigger than their stomachs—or at least so it seems. Incidentally wrangling perch while using an oversize presentation for larger gamefish isn't uncommon.

Perch fancy worms, invertebrates, and insect larvae that litter the lake bottom. But perch also have a penchant for crayfish. Working in unison, several perch might approach a larger crayfish and attack from different angles, picking, prodding, and plucking it apart piece by piece. After the crayfish's unfortunate demise, the school of perch moves on to find another target.

Perch commonly pester larger minnows, especially shiners and dace used for walleye and northern pike. Catching a perch when the large minnow becomes stuck in the fish's gullet proves that perch, at minimum, try to stretch their stomachs to the maximum when presented the opportunity.

Taking a cue from these overzealous eaters before reaching into the tackle box may prompt a sizable increase in lure selection. Identical offerings, but in larger suitable sizes, reflect more light, move more water when given action, and can be seen from a greater distance compared to smaller-size presentations.

Choosing a larger bait additionally increases the average size of caught fish. Fingerling perch attack small jigs and spoons like kamikazes, striking with fury and hanging themselves in the process. They grab on and shake their heads so rapidly and violently that it makes your rod tip quiver in Morse code as a fish inadvertently becomes hooked. If you've ever fished for perch and encountered little ones, you understand what I'm talking about. A single, small perch may be interested in your bait to some extent, but schools of dwarfs are relentless. Both hunger and competition fuel the activity. If one fish hits your minnow or larva and tears off only a small portion, another greedy perch is quick to latch onto the remainder.

Deepwater Perch

As the ice season progresses, perch begin gravitating toward deepwater ledges and basins. Depth is relative when considering small ponds in a regional locale compared to massive lakes that bottom out at over a hundred feet. While some fisheries retain perch at depths of 50 feet or more, "deep water" is disproportionate in lakes that max out at only 20 feet.

Perch inhabiting deep water don't wander aimlessly, but instead gravitate toward slight abnormalities in structure. Minor gradation in terrain is harder to locate compared to jutting points or a massive reef, but variations in bottom content, small pockets in the substrate, and subtle contour changes all attract deepwater perch. For instance, stringy clumps of vegetation the size of a kitchen table are attractive to deepwater perch no matter the weed type, because certain depths don't have much for vegetative growth. A palm tree in the desert is attractive because the land around is primarily barren. The palm tree provides some protection and acts as a point of reference. A perch's use of deepwater vegetation or other intricacies is equally justified. This can be initially troublesome for anglers trying to

find the slight variations attractive to deep perch, but the payoff is worth the effort. Again, contour information from paper or electronic maps is invaluable, referencing viable starting points to begin your quest for deepwater perch.

There's little variation between deep- and shallow-water perch presentations with the exception of weight. Fishing 30, 40, or 50 feet down requires a slight increase in the weight of your presentation, which can be accomplished by slightly larger jigs and spoons or by adding malleable split-shot onto the line. Without doing so, the angler loses sensitivity and contact with the bait. Monofilament's spirals that form from the shape of the reel spool over time create just enough slack to make bite detection difficult in deep water. Braided superline is a good choice in this situation because it doesn't stretch and resists the formation of "memory" from lying on the reel spool.

Perch on the Fringe

Locating winter perch isn't a guaranteed endeavor. Even lakes with surmountable populations don't have fish in every area. The usual flats, points, humps, and drop-offs are viable options, but one element can make the difference between a good day and a great day: the fringe.

Fringe is weeds. Fringe is gravel. Fringe is just about anything that comprises the bottom. In one respect, it is an area of transition. Weeds to silt. Muck to

■ Perch roaming deepwater areas hang around major structural elements like reefs and points, but gravitate toward minor subtleties, such as bottom content transitions, in certain lakes.

gravel. Sand to rock. In another, it's the most attractive area in the underwater world for plumper perch.

Fish are simply enamored with transition areas. Yet it's the fringe, the area where the substrate actually changes, that provides appeal. These locales offer the better of two worlds for hungry fish, offering access to two different cover or substrate types. Perch may feed upon insect larvae and bottom-dwelling worms within weeds, and then swim a few feet to encounter minnows or crayfish around rocks. These "fringe" locations also act as natural pathways for fish and forage to navigate. Acting as a point of reference, perch travel along the transition line, using the route to capitalize on consumption.

Both shallow- and deepwater fish congregate near fringe areas. Though weeds can make up one of the two or more elements comprising fringe in shallow water, encountering vegetation as a fringe component is rare in deep water. Light penetration depreciates at greater depths, prohibiting healthy weed growth from forming. Adding snow and ice as a light-blocking barrier during the winter months only compounds the situation. However, fringe still exists at these depths, but the elements involved are substrate related. Transitions from silt to clay, rock to sand, muck to gravel, and any other combination of changing bottom types attract schools of perch. A small spot of sand secluded in the middle of a silt-laden bottom is okay, but larger areas of differentiation are bet-

ter. If the zone is bigger than the footprint of your garage, we're talkin' business!

Locating fringe takes some time, but the return is worthwhile. You may already wonder how one systematically finds these transitions, but it's actually no different than the methods used for pinpointing weed lines.

A Vexilar flasher serves as your underwater eyes while searching for fringe. An underwater camera can also display well-defined transitions, but the time required to drop the camera and haul it back in makes the flasher more expedient, especially in deep water. Yet the camera allows positive identification of bottom type once the fringe is located.

Anglers understand the ease of using a flasher to show an ice fishing bait and present fish, but many fail to push the electronics to full capacity and utilizing sonar to determine bottom type. With a Vexilar FL-8, FL-18, FL-12, or FL-20 in hand, turn the gain up to a level much greater than used to effectively see a small bait. Then turn the range to more than double the depth you're fishing. The goal is to obtain a "double echo," indicating the presence of hard bottom. For example, if in 15 feet of water, a signal will appear at 15 feet and again at precisely double that depth, in this case 30 feet. Since sonar entails emitting a sound signal into the water then measuring the span required for it to bounce off the bottom and come back to the transducer, a hard substrate sends the sonar signal into hyperactivity. The sound bounces off the bottom and returns to the transducer, but additionally it ricochets off the bottom of the ice, reverberates back to the bottom of the lake, and finally reaches the transducer once again. The increase in gain level is required due to the weakened return of the double echo. Once one of these hard-bottom areas is found, begin augering holes to find the edge of the hard bottom. The display won't show a double echo when positioned over silt or mud, in this case the fringe between soft and hard bottom, your key to catching more and bigger perch!

CHAPTER NINE

Ice Fishing for Bluegill

Even though bluegill, often referred to as sunfish, are one of the smallest freshwater fish that anglers pursue, they remain wildly popular because of their sheer abundance and willingness to bite. Yet finding respectable-size bluegill remains challenging. Anglers won't catch bluegill in every area of the lake, even if high populations are available. But once a few fish are located, the probability of catching more is likely due in part to their social, schooling behavior.

Locating Winter 'Bulls

The pursuit for hard-water bluegill begins with a map and conversation. But catching abnormally huge bluegill, also known as 'bulls, is tricky. Some lakes that support a seemingly infinite supply of platter-size bluegill during the summer months seem to fall off the map in winter. Stubborn anglers can crack the code of missing-in-action bluegills if they dedicate themselves to the cause, but in all honesty there are plenty of highly populated bluegill lakes to entertain your attention and frying pan with less effort.

Bluegills are generally found in somewhat shallow environments during the first portion of the season. An abundance of oxygen and food draws the fish to the area, but not every shallow-water section has fish. A tip from the local bait shop might give you some generalities such as a specific lake and even depth, but now it's up to you to actually find the fish. Haphazardly setting up base in the suggested depth is a gamble.

Vegetation is the primary attractor when it comes to shallow-water structure, yet not all weeds are equally favored by bluegills. Different lakes have different weeds, but the majority contain a few general vegetative types that every angler should know about. Matted weeds protruding only a few inches from the bottom don't provide the cover bluegills need for ambushing small schools of transient minnows or hiding from larger predators. Commonly found in most shallow-water ecosystems, these stringy weeds of consistent height offer little diversity to attract bluegill or fish of any species.

Thick-stalked vegetation with broad leaves is a better alternative due to a higher

■ Chasing bluegills is an exciting quest, even though the fish is one of freshwater's smaller inhabitants. Tiny hooks and light line are essential for catching this species of sunfish.

likelihood of supporting forage in addition to its camouflaging properties. Large predators like northern pike, muskie, and largemouth bass have more difficulty identifying small mouthfuls of bluegill when interspersed among like-size leaves of similar shape.

Tight clumps of cylindrical-shaped weeds are another good option for sunfish. Frequently called "coontail" in northern regions because of its resemblance to a raccoon's fluffy tail, this aquatic plant grows in smaller groups, sometimes mixed in with other weed types. Bluegill gravitate toward isolated coontail clusters, but when it's interspersed with other plants, the draw is much greater. This is true for nearly every type of underwater vegetation. Diverse vegetation provides better cover for fish than a single weed class.

Green, healthy weeds tend to attract more fish than brown, decomposing vegetation. Finding healthy weeds is much easier during the first portion of the ice season, but depending on the lake, weeds can flourish throughout the winter. Conversely, some lakes never seem to develop crisp stalks or leaves. Somewhat dependent upon water clarity and quality, fish in these bodies of water settle for what's available, establishing residence in dense, yet deteriorating weeds.

Emergent weed types like lily pads and pencil reeds aren't nearly as desirable to panfish during the winter months compared to the open-water season. Drilling holes in large patches of reeds stretched above the snow cover yields little success during early ice and throughout the majority of the season. Yet when the sun's angle begins to focus more directly on the Earth in the latter part of the year, these unlikely areas gain potential.

As bluegill move back into shallow water as the ice deteriorates late in the season, emergent weeds act as mini solar panels, melting the ice around the perimeter of the stalks. These portholes permit access to the world above. Water from melting snow can seep down the open accesses, creating warmer pockets while oxygenating the lake environment. Catching bluegill in the center of shallow pencil reeds isn't likely for most of the winter, but bluegill gravitate toward those edges as the ice begins to melt, sitting just outside them looking for food within shallow, submergent weeds.

Bluegill in the Abyss

Some lakes and seasonal periods find bluegill occupying deep water. Basin-type areas attract bluegill via food and little else. Suspended plankton and bottom-dwelling invertebrates provide sustenance for deep-roaming schools of fish. Even though massive open-water areas provide little protection from larger predators, the availability of food circumvents a need for safety. Since bluegill gravitate toward deeper, forage-rich regions when shallow areas fail to offer necessary or equally abundant provisions, the attractiveness of shallow-water weed cover means little to the hungry panfish. Deepwater bluegills disperse throughout basins that max out at about 25 or 30 feet, but catching bluegill beyond this depth is a rarity. Soft, silt-rich bottoms attract schools of bluegill, much more so than sand or rock. The softer substrate provides the proper environment for the invertebrates that bluegill feast upon.

It's no secret that bluegill prefer to eat super-small presentations. Some of their primary food sources beneath the ice include organisms so minuscule they're difficult to detect by human sight. Ironically, using tackle that's too small for bluegill can prove problematic. It's actually more common for anglers to utilize oversize presentations. The body and profile of a jig that's too small for bluegill isn't of concern, but the hook is.

Hooks that aren't big enough won't securely hold a fish throughout the fight, and the ultra-thin wire can bend beneath a large bluegill. Very few companies produce

■ A tiny jig and maggot fooled this bruiser bluegill. Perhaps the most basic of panfish presentations, small jigs tipped with live bait emulate the look of miniature, naturally present food choices.

items that are actually "too small" for panfish, so you're pretty safe in leaning toward the smallest jigs you can find, but be well aware of the implications of super-small hooks when browsing the tackle aisles.

Basic Bluegill Bait

Jigs, jigs, so many jigs! As winter approaches and anglers tuck their boats beneath covers to hibernate until spring arrives, hunters swarm the woods in search of a diversion until the ice is thick enough for fishing once again. At the same time, tackle shops transform their shelves from bluewater specialties to ice fishing accoutrements. Because of the size of ice fishing equipment and its overall volume in comparison to open-water tackle, only a portion of a store supports ice angling products. Many of the items left over from summer dangle from pegboard hooks in adjacent aisles. Most of that equipment isn't necessary or applicable to ice fishing, especially when it comes to bluegill. Even the small feather, hair, or plastic-bodied jigs tossed for sunfish throughout the summer months do little to enhance your ice fishing action.

Ice jigs for bluegill weigh a fraction of their open-water counterparts. A $\frac{1}{16}$-ounce jig is too big to entice many bluegill during winter. Weights that are more common are $\frac{1}{64}$ to $\frac{1}{128}$ ounce, but don't be surprised if those numbers seem discordant when comparing two like-size jigs. The weights are derived by the manufacturer and aren't necessarily precise. Size

in terms of appearance becomes a better gauge, especially when considering jigs constructed of materials other than lead, since identical-size jigs composed of varying materials have different weights.

A good selection of teardrops, ants, and similar-size jigs of various origins are commonplace in the adept ice angler's tackle box. A hundred of these hooks are small enough to fit into a compact carrier that's easily transported in the oversize pockets of a cold-weather parka, and remain historically productive for panfish in general.

Providing appropriate action is equally important to presenting an appealing bait, and a few techniques shine no matter what lake you're fishing. Bluegill are attracted to activity, but when it comes to biting, a pause in the action takes the fish from looking to eating.

Gently jigging your presentation garners attention from nearby bluegills, but lifting the bait up high, then dropping it without tension often attracts bluegill from a wider range. This lift-and-drop technique is also deadly on big crappies and works best with the lightest ice jigs.

When you see bluegill visually in clear water or on the display of your flasher, a game of keep-away prompts more bites than swimming your bait toward the fish, which often scares them off for good. Moving your presentation horizontally away from a fish usually gets them to follow, but raising the presentation vertically is even more enticing. Many times the two movements in combination prompt the wary bluegill to bite.

Unconventional Bluegill Attractors

Even though sunfish can only eat a mouthful, their curious behavior is advantageous for anglers. Large spoons and even spearing decoys can attract schools of panfish, even though they have no chance of eating the oversize, flashy attractor.

Position the decoy or spoon high in the water column so the flash reflects from the bottom of the ice. Brightly colored wooden spearing decoys seem to work best, and finesse isn't necessary. After bending the tail to force its motion in a tight circle, pull hard on the cord. These tight, fast circles attract roaming schools of bluegill and even crappie. Dropping a small jig accompanied with live bait or a plastic trailer once the fish are within visible range prompts the curious bluegill to bite. Catching several fish as the school gradually disperses is common. The stragglers often join other roaming groups of fish that the angler can attract using the same methods.

Dropper Rigs

Combining the best of both worlds, a dropper rig incorporates a hookless spoon tied in line a few inches above a small ice jig. The spoon is used as the attractor, luring bluegill into close proximity from a distance. Once the fish realizes it cannot engulf the spoon, it turns to the tiny jig

trailing behind and chomps on the miniature morsel.

Frost-shot Bluegill

Anglers searching for panfish have always had to carefully experiment on each ice outing to find the perfect bait for the day, an equally proportional amount of flash and vibration paired with subtlety and finesse. An interesting presentation that combines both is the Frost-shot rig.

The Frost-shot is attached to your line the same way a drop-shot is configured for summer use. First, fasten a Lindy Genz Bug to 3-pound-test Berkley Micro Ice line using a Palomar knot, leaving a 12-inch tag end to tie on a large Lindy Frostee spoon with the treble hook removed. You can experiment on the distance allowed between the Genz Bug and the Frostee spoon, but it won't take long to find out that this rigging option catches fish.

The reason the Frost-shot works so well is due to a couple factors. First, it combines flash and vibration, produced via the Frostee spoon, with the subtlety and finesse of the Genz Bug. The rig also caters to the anatomical make-up of the fish you're chasing. Because fish have eyes positioned on either side of their heads, their ability to see in certain directions, such as beneath their bodies, is compromised, while looking vertically above them is a strength. The Frost-shot rig attracts panfish to close proximity with the flash of the Frostee spoon, and when the fish arrive, they can easily detect the Genz Bug

■ The Frost-shot rig pairs the flash of a jigging spoon with the subtlety of a tiny jig, creating the perfect combination to attract and catch big bluegill.

hovering above them within their field of vision.

Because the Genz Bug is suspended above the flashy Frostee spoon, it performs better than a dropper rig in which the spoon is tied in line above and the smaller jig is attached at the bottom of your main line. The movements of the jig are isolated, and the angler has much more control over its motion. Since the jig is tied on with the Palomar knot, every time the rod tip is jiggled, the Genz Bug moves in a hinged, rocking manner that works extremely well for undulating a waxworm, eurolarve, or soft plastic Lindy Munchies Tiny Tail as an artificial alternative.

Although this rig is created with similarities to a drop-shot rig, it's fished much differently. Drop-shot rigs originated for bass fishing during the open-water season, although slight adaptations make them a great choice for fish of all species. The use of a drop-shot rig is specific; cast the presentation to an area and let the weight sit on the bottom while gingerly lifting the rod tip to make the soft plastic bait situated above the sinker dance and shake, without ever bringing the bait closer to the boat. It essentially allows an angler to fish vertically in a horizontal situation (casting from a boat).

While ice fishing, the angler *is* vertical, so there really is no need to position a weight on the bottom to keep a bait from moving horizontally. But ice fishing, even with the advancements made to increase mobility, finds anglers trying to attract fish

toward the bait from the immediate vicinity. If that range increases and fish begin to approach from an even greater distance, then the chance of catching more and bigger fish rises.

The Frost-shot works great in three scenarios. First, and one that seems quite logical, is during low-light conditions. The period at dusk and after dark calls for more flash and so does the presence of muddy or stained water. The flash and vibration of the Frost-shot calls the fish in, and when you hit the Frostee's Techni-glo finish with a Tazer, the luminescent qualities simply add to its attraction.

Another prime scenario is in shallow water. Since fish don't have the same field of vision in super-shallow situations, the Frost-shot rig is much easier for fish to hear and feel, bringing them to close proximity.

The last scenario that calls for a Frost-shot is clear water. Even though fish can see much farther in clear water, we're still trying to increase the area from which we're attracting fish. In clear water, this area increases dramatically, and there's no better way to take advantage of that than by using the perfect balance of flash, vibration, subtlety, and finesse provided by the Frost-shot rig.

The Hammer Rig

A hammer rig is a derivative of the Frost-shot rig. The major difference is that the hammer rig uses a modified Lindy Genz Worm as the drop weight. Begin once more by tying a small jig onto your fishing line using a Palomar knot and leaving a long tag end. Again, the Lindy Genz Bug is a great choice for this because of its size and hook angle.

Using a wire cutter, clip the hook from the Genz Worm and use the remainder as the weight for the Frost-shot. Now bait up and drop down!

Concise jigging action makes the Genz Bug jiggle and dance while remaining somewhat isolated by the weight of the Genz Worm. So, why use the Genz Worm as the weight versus a flashier spoon? When fish are curious but not feeding gregariously, the smaller combination of baits offers a similar action to the Frost-shot rig, but without the massive appearance of a larger jigging spoon that could potentially frighten an apprehensive bluegill.

Slingshot

The slingshot is yet another modification of the Frost-shot rig. The difference is that the slingshot rig doesn't utilize a flashy spoon or even a colorful jig as an attractor. Instead, attach a tiny number 10 or 12 plain hook using the same Palomar knot required for the horizontal hook presentation of a Frost-shot rig. Then tie a surgeon's loop from the tag end of the remaining line. A few tiny split-shot pinched onto the loop provide the needed weight and act as mini-attractors at close range. Connecting the split-shot to the loop prevents them from sliding off a straight, loose line.

Since the slingshot is a super-finesse presentation, a very light line is required. To round out the package, slip a couple eurolarve or plastic-tails onto the hook.

Late-Ice Panfish

Finicky fish require subtlety, coercion, and an all-out finesse commitment to get some action. But the tides are now turning. As the days lengthen and the sun warms frozen expanses of water with greater intensity, fish become more willing to eat larger meals. In fact, they'll seek out bigger portions to satisfy an increasing appetite with less effort. From early March until ice-out, the metabolic rates of crappie and bluegill continually increase as their bodies yearn for nutrients, giving both species reason to feed intensely for long periods of time.

The spawn is months away, but the preparation process has already begun, and these panfish require more food to function at an optimal level, taking in the nutrients critical for final development of their 50,000 (bluegill) to over 100,000 (crappie) eggs. Anglers wanting to capitalize on this period of increased activity should make it a priority to get on the ice.

Late ice becomes a time of transition; the snow has melted, auger holes actually expand instead of freezing over, and environmental changes that ultimately lead to open water directly impact the fish.

Water produced from melting snow and ice begins seeping through any open crevice, creating warm flowages that attract fish because of the increased water temperature and unified supply of miniature cuisine including ice fleas and ice spiders. Fish that once adhered to the bottom have now taken flight, floating purposefully close to the underside of the lake's icy sheath. These fish are at the height of activity, jockeying for position to get first crack at a meal.

Locating eager biters requires effort equal to that put forth during any ice excursion, but the late ice period tends to give panfish reason to situate themselves higher in the water column compared to their midwinter haunts, which amplifies the differences between vertical and horizontal fish location.

This adds an interesting component to the day: sight-fishing. Traditionally achieved by angling through a large spearhole in a dark house, sight-fishing can also be accomplished by staring into an outdoor ice hole face-first. Peering through the water while lying on your belly might

■ **When bluegill become aggressive, larger presentations such as jigging spoons catch the big ones, leaving smaller fish to the anglers utilizing conventional tiny hooks.**

sound cold, wet, and uncomfortable, but the technique does work. Rapid reflexes are imperative since body repositioning is essential upon hook-set. You can't simply reel the fish up to your face!

There is, however, an alternative to soaking your britches, brought on by warm spring temperatures. As bluegill reposition higher in the water column to intercept food, warm water, and oxygen, they are easily visible to the angler, even from a standing posture. Bluegill cruising only a few feet below the ice may be easy to see, but aren't guaranteed to bite.

Seeing fish is advantageous. Recognizing fish presence places more emphasis on proper technique while simultaneously reviving an angler's level of concentration. But, realize that "buck fever" can quickly set in when staring down at an oversize bluegill. This is the time to take control and begin "playing" with the fish. Purposefully moving your bait away from the fish prompts them to actively follow and subsequently attack.

A well-stocked tackle box will already possess miniature jigging favorites, and tipping the hook with a grub is sure to put a keeper on the ice, but because these fish are so aggressive, your best bet may still be sitting on the shelf at the tackle shop.

Artificial and all-natural minute imitators allow you to catch more fish between threading on attractors, and maximize your time on the lake, keeping your hands in your gloves instead of your waxworm box.

Lindy's line of soft plastic-tails may not look identical to a waxworm, but after seeing one dance, wiggle, and vibrate extended from the end of a jig, you'll agree that their unique attractive qualities will get the fish excited. There's no messy sawdust, and the Lindy Munchies won't die if they freeze!

Another alternative to live bait is Berkley's all-natural Gulp! maggots. These tiny morsels put 400 percent more scent into the water compared to traditional plastic baits and are biodegradable. They remain one of my favorites for icing big perch, crappies, and bluegills.

CHAPTER TEN

Other Species under the Ice

Although the various fish species highlighted in this chapter aren't often sought out by all ice anglers, they are undoubtedly a challenge to locate and catch. Remember, if a fish puts a bend in the pole, no matter the species, it's an enjoyable battle.

Bass

Many people ignore bass after the water turns from liquid to solid, yet anglers catch some of the year's largest bass during this period.

Finding success catching largemouth through the hard-water season is achievable, but don't expect the numbers to compare to summer catches. A handful of fish would deem an outing successful, although ten to fifteen-fish mornings are possible, especially during late ice. Because the fish's metabolism drops substantially as the water drops below 50 degrees, finding a window of opportunity when the bass are feeding can be difficult. Yet, just as human beings differ in their metabolic rates, so do bass. Some will eat only one meal in the course of a month, while others will feed more aggressively.

To find winter largemouth, locate areas of cabbage weed and coontail adjacent to a drop-off with access to deep water. Productive water can be as shallow as 5 or 6 feet, but typically 8 to 15 feet is best. You will find that crappie and bluegill and, of course, predatory pike inhabit areas such as these, but they also hold populations of largemouth bass.

The most important aspect to keep in mind is that you don't fish bass through the ice like you do during the open-water season. A jig and pig will not work! A Lindy Rattl'r or Flyin' Rattlr' spoon tipped with one waxworm is a better choice. Don't jerk the bait hard, but instead shake it in an attempt to wiggle the worm, not the body of the spoon. Keep the motion of the rod tip confined to an area less than half an inch. I know what you're thinking—a 20-inch bass eating a ½-inch maggot? The beauty of it is that the fish see the bait as a whole, and the flashing white of the worm looks like the belly of a minnow as it flips and twists, similar to an injured baitfish. Salmo Chubby Darters

■ Although bass aren't the typical target for ice anglers, occasional encounters while fishing for other species is a bonus. However, some anglers specifically look for bass beneath the ice, a viable endeavor if you know the procedure.

are also good winter bass lures as they have great vibration through the water.

Anglers looking for smallmouth bass won't experience much success when probing likely largemouth areas. Whereas largemouth prefer weeds and other structures protruding from the bottom, smallmouth devote themselves to depth variations in conjunction with a hard substrate. Throughout three seasons, smallmouth bass most prominently populate rock, gravel, and sand breaks, points, and humps, but winter finds exceptions. The greatest majority of smallmouth congregate in deepwater pools, establishing residence for the entire winter season. Though walleye anglers sometimes encounter smallmouth, their activity levels decrease over the winter months. With lowered metabolism, smallmouth expend less energy and thus take in less food. Yet when you find schools of fish, the likelihood of capture is high because the area tightly confines so many fish.

Minnows and their artificial imitators are suggested for winter smallmouth, but keeping the bait within the bottom half of the water column garners the most fish. Smallmouth aren't shy about tackling surface lures in open water, but the cold, dark atmosphere beneath the ice provokes smallies to lie low over the winter.

Rainbow Trout

With colors of the sunset emblazoned on their sides, rainbow trout cruise, hopeful for food. Their transient lifestyle leaves anglers in pursuit, chasing the fish as they move or patiently waiting for them to arrive.

Rainbows, however, are susceptible to angler harvest during the winter months, prompting wildlife officials to dub certain lakes off-limits to rainbow trout fishing through the ice. Often cruising in small schools just below the ice, the wandering fish look for minnows, insects, and zooplankton to sate their palates.

Trout don't set up on traditional lake structures like walleye, pike, or crappie, but instead prefer to glide over deep water or rotate around the perimeter of the lake. Since many lakes containing rainbow trout are small, anglers are able to canvass the body of water within a couple trips.

Some lakes have prominent populations of trout cruising in 20 to 50 feet of water, commonly positioned in the upper third of the water column. Other lakes find rainbow trout in shallow water, as the fish explore weedy edges and shallow flats in pursuit of forage. Schools will actually circle small lakes, and you can literally set a clock to their multiple daily arrivals. There's a great likelihood that you will find rainbow trout inhabiting both of these areas on a single lake.

Anglers in the mood for some rainbow trout action benefit from small, flashy spoons and small jigs tipped with live bait. Be sure to check local regulations for each body of water, since some designated trout lakes regulate the use of live minnows.

When tipped with a waxworm, minnow head, or small artificial attractor, small

■ This hefty rainbow trout fell prey to a jigging spoon lowered just below the ice. The aggressive nature of rainbow trout beneath the ice provides entertainment for anglers who venture onto lakes bearing the species.

spoons are a rainbow trout favorite. When fished just below the ice, the spoon reflects from the bottom of the ice cap, giving the illusion of a small school of baitfish. Shaking the spoon and violently ripping the lure both invite trout to approach. And once a fish strikes, you'll agree that they are one of the hardest-fighting freshwater fish around.

Another approach that garners rainbows is a simple jig and waxworm. Lindy's Genz Worm sits horizontal to the bottom, and a wad of waxworms or eurolarve stitched onto the hook looks tasty to trout.

Electronics are a must for any serious trout angler, since deep water requires major adjustments in presentation depth. Noticing a rainbow trout swimming 20 feet below your jig indicates the need for modification, but without a flasher to aid in your underwater observation, the task is hopeless.

Lake Trout

Professional angler Ron Anlauf knows a thing or two about lake trout. He dreams about the big fish year-round, and once the winter trout season opens, Anlauf emerges from the banks in search of huge lakers.

Anlauf admits that chasing lake trout is an obsessive quest. "There's a real rush to be had when you go toe-to-toe with a big laker through the ice, and the result is addicting. It's more than just the battle, though; it's everything that goes with it, like the beauty of a remote Canadian lake,

being all by yourself at times, and drilling holes where no man has previously ventured."

In winter, lake trout are at the pinnacle of activity, chasing schools of bait in gin-clear water. They frequently use the ice to their advantage, pushing schools of bait toward the barrier for easy capture. Because of this, anglers should watch their electronics but occasionally peer down the hole, since super-clear water permits a lake trout hunter the ability to see the fish initially circle, then engulf the bait.

Anlauf examines main-lake points with sheer drops into deep water when trying to locate lake trout. The fish prefer deep water, and it is common to encounter lake trout in 100 feet of water, but the 40- to 60-foot range seems most desirable for numbers and size.

While lake trout prefer fast drops against prominent main-lake structures, their nomadic lifestyle requires anglers to stay mobile. Spending a half hour or so in an area is all it takes to discover the presence of fish. If there's no action within that time, move on.

Live bait tempts lake trout, but it is unnecessary in most cases. Plastic tubes and horizontally moving lures are more than enough to elicit a strike. Anlauf prefers big, white tubes while employing a specific technique.

"The basic jigging tactic includes lifting the bait and letting it drop, and then waiting for it to settle out before raising it again. The tube will swim out on the

■ Professional angler Ron Anlauf shows off a monster lake trout caught north of the Canadian border. His successful tactics include artificial bait, such as plastic tubes, jigged aggressively over deep **water.** RON ANLAUF

upswing, and then turn back and glide back in on the drop. If you're getting stared down, you might try giving the bait a short pop or quiver, or keep doing what you're doing, whatever it takes. Fish will come in and not always take the bait right away, but if you can keep working them higher and higher, you just might get them to go," remarks Anlauf.

Stout gear is essential for lake trout, and heavier walleye rods are well suited for battle. Spooling up with braided superline is advantageous when targeting the colossal depths where lake trout lurk due to the braid's sensitivity, courtesy of its non-stretch characteristics. A few feet of 10- to 12-pound monofilament or fluorocarbon attached to the end as leader material makes your tether nearly invisible to weighty lakers swimming in pristine waters.

Muskie

The perception of muskie has changed greatly over the years, and the fish is gaining protection throughout ice fishing regions for a few reasons. First, the migratory patterns of muskellunge in rivers and smaller lakes is predictable in late fall and early winter, leaving the fish vulnerable to anglers. Catching a muskie in itself is the goal of many anglers, but mishandling the large fish can be detrimental to release and subsequent survival.

Exposure to extremely cold temperatures can quickly freeze fins and gills, and abrasive ice and snow rubs the protective slime from their sides, causing a higher occurrence of infection and ultimately proving fatal to big fish.

Anglers must exhibit great caution when pursuing muskie in permitted regions. Warm days cause less stress to fish, so muskie aficionados should carefully select their anticipated angling days.

When fishing for muskie through the ice, equipment and techniques mirror those employed for big pike. Both tip-ups and handheld rod and reel outfits have the capacity to wrangle muskie, but because their jaws are so strong and lined with long, razor-sharp teeth, heavy line and a leader are essential.

Muskies have little inhibition in taking a large presentation. Minnows of 10 inches or more are an easy meal for muskie. Big spoons and swimming lures additionally gain interest from the aggressive creatures.

Location is also quite similar in comparison to northern pike, and the two species often share locales. Weedy flats and drop-offs, rock piles, humps, points, bottleneck areas, and deepwater holes all potentially hold muskie. Incidental pike are caught frequently while muskie fishing, keeping your hopes alive for catching the "fish of 10,000 casts."

Tullibee

Even though tullibee aren't wildly popular, their beauty is attractive to anglers who accidentally encounter the silver-sided

freshwater fish and for those who purposefully chase the oversize minnows. Few anglers fry up a load of tullibee, but instead smoke the oily fish over woody coals.

Tullibee and its close relative, the whitefish, act as forage to large predators like walleye, northern pike, muskie, and lake trout. Lakes containing tullibee and whitefish commonly have high gamefish numbers and size, due to the beneficial forage base provided by the fish that range in size up to a maximum of about four or five pounds.

Anglers looking for tullibee really cannot fish too deep. Their flexible biology allows them to roam great expanses without feeling the effects of pressure changes brought on by rapid changes in depth.

During the early part of the ice fishing season, tullibee roam the perimeter of basins, slightly shallower than normal, looking for zooplankton, insects, and small minnows. Stalling along defined structures like points, bars, and distinct weed protrusions, anglers catch early-season tullibee

■ Tullibee gravitate toward the flash of a jigging spoon and gobble up small jigs accompanied by live bait. Because of this, anglers looking to catch walleye, perch, crappie, and bluegill incidentally catch a few tullibee when fishing lakes containing the silver-sided species.

using panfish techniques and presentations. A waxworm covering the hook of a small jig or a tiny spoon paired with a worm or crappie minnow head are craved menu items.

As the ice season progresses, tullibee action slows, intensifying again as the days become longer and the ice begins to deteriorate. Fish once again travel the perimeter of bays and basins, but numbers of tullibee stack up in the basin holes. This deepwater bite requires the use of a flasher, since fish continually arrive and depart at varying depths.

A Final Thought

The best ice anglers, no matter what species they chase, remain flexible in thought and action. Some crazy ideas have turned into common ice fishing practice. The only way to determine what will or will not actually work involves constant experimentation. Whether you have inspiration for customizing your four-wheeler to haul your ice fishing gear proficiently or plan to employ a new technique or bait, take the initiative to follow through with your plan. Although ice fishing has changed dramatically over the past twenty-five years, some of the best ideas for improving gear and angling success might still be waiting for discovery. So put this book on the shelf, grab your ice auger, and go fishing!

About the Author

Jason Durham is a professional angler and fishing guide who takes classic ice fishing ideas and turns them into innovative approaches, honing his skills around his hometown of Park Rapids, Minnesota, an epicenter of ice fishing activity with nearly a hundred lakes within a 10-mile radius.

"Our ice fishing season typically runs from Thanksgiving to mid-April, giving anglers plenty of time to catch nearly every species of freshwater fish from a hard-water vantage point," Durham says.

Durham owns and operates Go Fish! Guide Service, entertaining clients from around the globe. He shares angling techniques firsthand through guiding and instructional seminars, and writes fishing columns for numerous magazines and newspapers, offering insights to help others catch more fish.

In addition to educating anglers, Durham educates children, teaching kin-

dergarten in Nevis, Minnesota, a small school district in the northern portion of the state.

Pro Tactics: Ice Fishing is Jason Durham's second book in the Pro Tactics™ Series. His first, *Pro Tactics: Panfish* is available online and in bookstores nationwide.